Stop Playing Games!

A Project Manager's Guide
to Successfully Navigating
Organizational Politics

By Rick A. Morris

RMC
Publications, Inc.

Printed in the United States of America

First Printing

ISBN: 978-1-932735-39-0

Library of Congress Control Number: 2010936373

"PMP" and "PMI" are marks of the Project Management Institute, Inc. "Microsoft" and "SharePoint" are registered trademarks of Microsoft Corporation in the United States and/or other countries. "Whac-a-Mole" is a registered trademark of Bob's Space Racers, Inc.

RMC
Publications, Inc.

Phone: 952.846.4484
Fax: 952.846.4844
E-mail: info@rmcproject.com
Web: www.rmcproject.com

Dedication

This book is dedicated to my wife Stephanie, daughter Ramsey, and son Remo. Thank you for always reminding me what all of this is for.

To my fellow project managers, the time has come. Be prepared to be the strategic resource that will be the differentiator between long-lasting success and failure for many organizations. It is time for a new era of project management.

ACKNOWLEDGMENTS

First and foremost, I would like to thank my family: my lovely wife, Stephanie, who through her hard work and perseverance enables me to follow my dreams; my daughter, Ramsey, who teaches me every day how to be a better person; and my son, Remo, who keeps me laughing and on my toes.

I would like to thank Laurie, Mary, Whitney, Deborah, Erica, Eric, Tim, and the entire RMC Project Management team for believing in me and helping pull together a wonderful project!

Finally, I would like to thank my business partner and friend, Greg Huffman, for all that he does and the commitment to making R^2 Consulting a continued success.

TABLE OF CONTENTS

ABOUT THE AUTHOR

Rick A. Morris, PMP, is an ITIL Practitioner, consultant, author, mentor, and creator of a foundation to promote Project Management in charities and other non-profits. Rick is an accomplished project manager and public speaker. His appetite for knowledge and passion  for the profession make him an internationally sought-after speaker at PMI® chapters and civic organizations, and a frequent guest lecturer at universities. He holds the Project Management Professional (PMP®), MPM (Masters of Project Management), OPM3, Six Sigma Green Belt, MCITP, MCTS, MCSE, TQM, ATM-S, ITIL, and ISO certifications. Rick is the Owner of R^2 Consulting, LLC. He has worked for organizations such as GE, Xerox, and CA and has consulted for numerous clients in a wide variety of industries including financial services, entertainment, construction, non-profit, hospitality, pharmaceutical, retail, and manufacturing.

Rick has two previous books (*The Everything Project Management Book, 2nd Edition*, published by Adams Media, and *Project Management That Works*, published by AMACOM), which were released in 2008. He is an active member of the Project Management Institute, is a graduate of the 2010 PMI® Leadership Masters Class, and has served in many leadership positions for PMI® chapters.

Rick is no stranger to being center stage in front of large groups of people. At the early age of 11, Rick was a Walt Disney World Performer in their seasonal shows. In high school, he worked at MGM Studios on various projects including the New Mickey Mouse Club. Taking the experience of his youth and blending it with the knowledge he attained throughout his career, Rick has inspired and mentored thousands of project managers. His blend of real-world experience and down-to-earth delivery style makes his passion for project management contagious.

FOREWORD

I really like this book, and I like even more where Rick Morris is coming from.

When I started teaching and consulting in project and team management in the mid-1970s, most of the "project managers" we worked with were victims of the now famous Peter Principle.

As described in their timeless book, *The Peter Principle* (William Morrow & Co., Inc., 1969), Raymond Hull and Peter Laurence proposed that in any technical profession (e.g., engineering, chemistry, teaching, IT), people would be promoted for their technical skills until a barrier was reached where the organization could not face paying higher salaries for technical work. The solution was to promote them to a position of management where the higher salary could be justified. As a result, many of the early project managers were technical people promoted to a position that no longer required their technical training. Instead, they needed people and administrative management skills. Hence, we have the Peter Principle, which argues that many people are promoted to "one level above their level of competence."

As project management continues its growth from a semi-profession to a true profession, assisted by the rise of the Project Management Institute and other similar bodies throughout the world, many new project managers are now facing a subtle, but critical, update of the Peter Principle.

In my book, *People and Project Management* (published in 1979, now out of print), I argued that project management was not about GANTT charts and percent complete models. Instead, *project management is about managing creative people*. That statement is even more resonant in 2010.

What you will find in Rick Morris's book are some powerful, perhaps slightly subversive, insights into the real world of managing the complex projects of the 21st century. Even if you are managing small projects, the complexity of establishing, building, and maintaining relationships with stakeholders, sponsors, colleagues, and team members is just as challenging on a small project as it is on a larger one.

You see, what Rick is really saying in this book is that while project management tools, techniques, and practices are very important, what is really important is people—specifically, the conversations, communication, and behaviors that people choose to have and choose to exhibit.

In *Stop Playing Games!*, Rick states that "A project manager should spend from 90 to 95 percent of his or her time communicating on the project." This statement is absolutely true. My small consulting group has observed hundreds of projects around the world. Many of these have either failed or have run into serious trouble. In almost every case, two principal factors determined the fate of these projects.

The first was a failure in the communication and behavior of the sponsor, critical stakeholders, and project manager *before* the project started. False expectations, badly researched estimates of benefits and costs with little or no data to support them, and poor scoping all condemned the project to an often long path to failure. As I stated in my book *Radical Project Management* (2003), "most projects that fail, fail before they started."

The second, and perhaps more serious, cause of failure was a lack of *professional* behavior from the project manager. Rather than following professional approaches to estimation and other project management practices, asserting their position as a project manager, and using effective negotiation of project constraints, the project manager was agreeing to unrealistic expectations and fell into a behavior that we have seen hundreds of times. As Rick says, "When speaking to project managers, they express a common theme of being a victim or powerless."

As a project management consultant and teacher for over 40 years, I have often thought of changing my business card from reading "Agile Project Management Consultant" to "Observer of Human Behavior." The truth is that a great project manager is not only a great observer of human behavior but a great changer of human behavior.

That is the Peter Principle issue facing many contemporary project managers. They have been promoted because they have learned basic project management theory and practice. However, we will all learn eventually that people cannot simply be "read about."

To understand people, you have to understand behavior, its causes, its impact, and more importantly, how to confront it when it is negative. You need to understand how to turn it into a positive force that assists the project manager and the team in achieving the dream.

Throughout this book, Rick moves from advice about practical project management tools and techniques to advice about the more difficult and less-explored area of behaviors or games. His advice is relevant, sound, and practical.

I hope you will enjoy this book as I did, smile at familiar scenes that all project managers face, and think and reflect about the true nature of project management in order to advance the profession as a whole.

Rob Thomsett

Consulting Director
The Thomsett Company p/l
Sydney, Australia

The Status of Our Profession

Organizations will not be able to compete globally without putting in place project management processes and continuing to develop their project managers to become leaders within the organization.

– Gina Westcott, Director of Management Development Programs, Boston University

The big raids will be for project management staff, so you need to ensure these staff are content.

– Philip Virgo, EURIM Secretary General

Project management is one of the most sought-after, yet misunderstood, professions in existence. It seems that every organization is searching for a strong project manager and is convinced it needs one—until it gets one! And it's not just organizations that do not understand what project management really involves. For the last 30 years, the project management profession has been struggling to find an identity, and its practitioners often find themselves searching for answers to questions like, *"What is project management?"* *"What value does it provide?"* *"How do I perform project management in organizations that do not believe in the principles of project management?"* and, *"Why am I a project manager?"*

Project management is expected to bend both time and space, yet two of the biggest blockers to the success of project management are (1) the lack of appreciation of the skills required of a competent project manager, and (2) the unwillingness of organizations to allow the qualified project manager to follow the process— from taking the time to develop accurate estimates, to identifying potential threats and opportunities, to creating a project management plan that is bought-into, approved, realistic, and formalized. Project managers have been forced to accept project constraints that have no basis in reality and that are often set at the whims of management. It's no wonder the CHAOS Report and other studies indicate such a high failure rate (as high as 82 percent) for projects.

Well, it is time for a new era. The era of reality. The era that rewards organizations for facing the decisions that cause projects to fail and eliminating the games that have evolved as a result. Welcome to the new era of project management!

To understand where this profession is going, we must first look at the current status of the profession. How did we get here? Why is this profession so misunderstood?

The answer lies with two key items. The first item is to answer the question, "How did you get into project management?" Was it the halo effect...gone wild?

THE HALO EFFECT...GONE WILD!

The halo effect means a perceptual bias where we assume that because a person is good at one thing, he or she must be good at others. For example, since a person is a great developer, he or she would make a great manager of a development project. To see the halo effect in action, ask how many project managers started their careers wanting to be project managers. The result is a very small percentage. Of course, project management is offered as a career path at only a few universities, so it may be a bit unfair to rate this as a halo effect. Yet many organizations and companies select project managers based on the other skills they possess.

During the research for this book, 200 project managers from various industries were asked how they became project managers. Of those polled, 161 of them (80.5 percent) reported that they were selected to run a project while they were employed in another role and continued managing projects thereafter. Only eight of those who answered the survey stated that they asked to become, or started their careers as, project managers.

Where do you fit? Project management can be one of the most rewarding careers in the marketplace, but it requires a tremendous balance of management techniques and political savvy. It is not a job that just anyone can do, contrary to popular opinion.

This brings us to the second item: not everybody can be a project manager. To rephrase this, anybody can be called a project manager, but not everyone will succeed as a project manager.

NOT EVERYBODY CAN BE A PROJECT MANAGER!

The belief that anyone can do project management is hindering the growth of the profession. Statistics are published that show an astounding percentage of projects that fail. But what these statistics rarely indicate is who is running the failing projects. Since unqualified people are being entrusted to do the work of a project manager, too many projects fail, and the project management profession faces an uphill battle to prove the value of project management. For some reason, even though there are many parallels to other professions, project management is not given the same status.

Do you think a chief financial officer (CFO) of an organization would walk up to a second-year employee and ask him or her, "Did you finish high school math? Great! We are short-handed in accounting and I need someone to help close the books!" Isn't accounting just math? It is just debits and credits, right? All you need to know is how to add and subtract. This is obviously not the case. Accounting is a specialized profession that requires education, practice, and thoroughness to do the job correctly. There are accounting certifications, and the profession requires constant reinforcement and education in new laws and regulations. Accounting is not something you would trust to just anybody.

How about another example? Let's look at insurance actuaries. This is a highly skilled profession requiring a tremendous amount of research and analysis. Essentially, actuaries determine the classes and rates for insurance companies to price their products. To oversimplify the profession, they are legalized gamblers. Of course, this is a jest. Actuaries perform an intensive amount of investigation to determine risk. For life insurance products, they assess health histories, morbidity tables, and large amounts of data to statistically group potential customers into categories. The hope is that the revenue generated from insurance premiums will be more than the insurance company has to pay out in claims. Do you think a CEO would walk up to an actuary and say, "I need to get a budgetary figure. Just throw me a number. I won't hold you to it!" Yet this is done to project managers on a daily basis.

It can be frustrating for project managers to work in a profession that is devalued so often. I'll say it again—it is time for a new era. It is time for organizations to choose professional project managers and allow them to follow the process and use the practices that they have been trained to use. If the ability to add and subtract does not make one an accountant, and guessing when someone is going to die does not make one an actuary, then creating an activity list and holding a status meeting does not make one a project manager!

IT TAKES MORE THAN ACTIVITY LISTS...

Project management is much more than creating and prioritizing a list of activities. In this new era, project managers need to apply a more sophisticated and comprehensive version of project management. Their personality style is important, too. The profession requires an even temper, phenomenal communication skills, and the ability to influence in all directions, especially if the project manager reports to the janitor on one project and then the CEO of an organization on the next project. Influencing in all directions means a project manager must understand the needs of his or her sponsor, understand the constraints of the project, and present options to the sponsor, while satisfying the needs of the team and stakeholders. In essence, it means the project manager is the interpreter, collector, and sender of information for multiple inputs and outputs. This is not an easy job!

Unfortunately, project managers rarely get a chance to even begin the process before they are asked to circumvent their training. Most projects that fail do so within the first five minutes of their existence. This is because many project managers accept the executive's directive at face value. When a project is assigned to the project manager with the constraints that it must be done by June 15th for a cost of $100,000, many practicing project managers are likely to simply accept the instruction and move on, assuming that because the executive said it, the budget is fixed and the date is fixed.

While there are times this may be true, it should be the exception, not the rule. Instead of mandating time and cost constraints, the sponsor should say something like, "Let me know as soon as possible whether you think this can be done by June 15th for $100,000, and if not, tell me what our options are." This statement communicates what the sponsor desires but also makes it clear that the organization is willing to be flexible for the right reason. If this statement is not made, and the project manager does not realize he or she might have an option beyond simply accepting the directive, then many times the project is doomed to fail. Let me share an example.

A large bank was implementing a new platform solution for all of its employees. When the project was assigned, the CEO stated that he wanted the project completed by the end of the year. Everybody nodded their heads, did not say another word, and then started working on the project. The organization felt that there was not enough time to plan the project and that the team should just get going. The "project manager" selected was one of the

CEO's favorite department managers. The CEO believed she was a fantastic choice to lead the effort.

Now fast-forward nine months. The project was not going well. The project manager was afraid to tell the CEO the current status. She believed she could turn the project around in time. The project team was disjointed and demoralized because, although they were working diligently, they did not seem to be making any progress. Almost every person on the project team knew the project would fail. That information was not making it back to the CEO, however. Since the CEO had heard that the project was going well, at the end of September he announced to stockholders the plans for the new platform and reported that it would be live at the end of December. Now the company was committed. In order to make the date, the team agreed that they would roll out the new platform on December 31 with the instructions, "Please do not use this software yet." This way they could say to the CEO that the project went live on the date promised.

When the project team was surveyed, they were asked if they thought this was really the result the CEO wanted. Astoundingly, almost all of them said it was. A couple of them said that they were pretty sure the CEO wanted it to work, but if he said December 31, he meant December 31. Obviously, this is not what the CEO wanted. There was a crucial moment when this became a project that needed to hit a deadline to save face. That moment was at the stockholder meeting in September. The team knew the project was doomed to fail long before then, but the CEO had not been given this information.

This story illustrates many errors that occur in project management. First, the wrong person was selected to be the project manager. Although she was a fantastic manager of a department, she did not have the skills to manage people outside of her direct influence (the halo effect in action!). Second, the dates were mandated to a point, but there was no analysis by the project manager and the team to determine if these dates were, in fact, achievable before the project work began. Third, the project manager and team failed to report the true project status to the CEO. Finally, the team was hoping for a miracle on every play, hoping to score, when they needed a more methodical game plan. The unfortunate part of this story is that such scenarios occur in almost every major company.

To bring this story back to the value of project management, many times sponsors, executives, or organizations do not see the value because all they are asking project managers to do is execute poor decisions! And many project managers do not push back against unrealistic directives and expectations. Some do not realize they can or should; for others, their organizational culture does not allow much room for push back. Project managers often do not have the ability to select or influence the date, budget, or requirements of the project. The project manager may not have the skill set to understand what he or she is missing. Then the company looks at the project manager and the missed result and concludes that there is no value in project management. This practice is one that must change in order for businesses to realize the real results that are attainable through project management.

AN ALTERNATIVE TO APATHY OR ACCEPTANCE OF THE MEDIOCRE

There are a tremendous number of project managers who are frustrated because they have been trained in a process that they know works, but the constraints of the organization do not allow them to use the process. This book will teach much more than theories of how to become successful in project management. It will discuss how to maximize the value of project management and provide real-world ways to stop playing the games that continue to devalue the profession of project management. The real-world tips and techniques presented in this book will help to create a common understanding between executives and project managers and help companies and organizations that do not value the process of project management begin to understand why the process is what it is.

The reasons projects fail have not changed since the project management industry started tracking the causes. Neither have the ways to prevent common causes of failure. The goal of the techniques within this book is to expose the flawed thinking in a constructive manner that allows for the education of management and the implementation of proper processes. As an example, let's look at the process of risk management. A simplistic view of the process, as we are taught it, is:

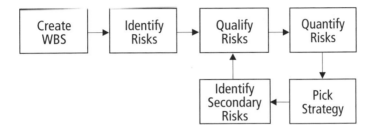

However, in most companies, the process is more like this:

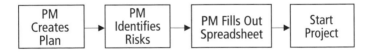

This is an oversimplification of the issue, but it illustrates what happens in thousands of organizations. Here are some actual quotes from sponsors and stakeholders on projects:

- *"This project has no risk, because it must be done on time."*
- *"We don't believe in work breakdown structures here."*
- *"Our organization does not allow you to use PERT."*

Unfortunately, you probably have heard some of these as well. So what can you do about it? Assuming the following is true, the rest of this book will help you learn techniques to improve the situation:

- You understand the process of project management, or, if you have not learned the proper process, you will.

- You believe in the process of project management and understand what it takes to create a proper and realistic project management plan.

- You will not accept status quo or failure as a norm.

- You truly believe that with the right techniques, one person (namely you) can make a difference in your organization!

To be clear, the intention of this book is not to shortcut or bypass any of the standard project management processes. Instead, it offers defined and tested techniques to help individuals influence their organizations to stop playing games and to start reaping the rewards proper project management can bring.

Are you ready to help usher in the new era of project management? Read on!

Finding Value in Project Management

2

Virtually every company will be going out and empowering their workers with a certain set of tools, and the big difference in how much value is received from that will be how much the company steps back and really thinks through their business processes...thinking through how their business can change, how their project management, their customer feedback, their planning cycles can be quite different than they ever were before.

– Bill Gates, Founder of Microsoft®

What is the value of project management? This can be a difficult question to answer. There is quite a bit of research and rhetoric in the business community that says project management is needed to achieve the results company stakeholders require. Yet some companies abandon all principles of project management at their earliest opportunity. How can you measure the value of a process that is not allowed to occur? A commonly heard phrase in corporate environments is, "We do not have time to plan; we have to get started!" However, at the end of another failed project, they cite a lack of planning as a key lesson learned. In the next project, the rush to get started persists. This is a downward cycle that must be broken.

WHY IS IT DIFFICULT TO ARTICULATE VALUE?

There have been many studies undertaken to determine the value of project management, including a multiyear study completed by the Project Management Institute (PMI®) that measured how organizations have benefited from project management. The results of this study state that there appears to be value, both tangible and intangible, but the actual value varies by company. For instance, some companies may see a tangible benefit of improved project predictability, while other companies may experience completely different benefits. What we can take away from this study is essentially that the value of project management is different for each organization. This result appears to be a bit vague and does not seem to really answer the question. Upon further reflection, however, the study is not flawed, and the answer is not flawed either. Instead, what is lacking is a common definition of a project.

What is a project? A technical response is that a project has a definitive beginning and end and produces a unique service, product, or result. Now, what is a project in your organization? The answers can be wide-ranging. Some companies have definitions such as, "anything over

40 hours," or, "anything that costs more than $50,000." These types of definitions generally create more projects than there are people to work on them. Such definitions also contribute to the high rates of project failure. So much time is spent trying to follow the process on so many projects that the resources become stretched too thin and the process is never allowed to finish. How can the value of project management be measured if the definition of a project is so arbitrary? How can quality project management be performed with ratios of 40 projects to one project manager?

The PMI® study also found that 60 percent of the executives surveyed felt their organizations needed to be better at project execution. However, the study does not indicate what percentage of those executives also believed their organization did an adequate job of planning. So many times the result of a project is failure, and the cause appears to be in the execution of the project. But what about the status of the plan? Was there a plan? Did failure occur in the execution of the project, or was it actually in the inception?

Dr. James Norrie published a more comprehensive study and result in the book *Breaking through the Project Fog* (J. Wiley & Sons Canada, 2008). Dr. Norrie articulates that the value of project management is directly proportional to the time at which the project manager becomes involved in the project. The earlier the project manager has the opportunity to assist in the definition of the scope, budget, and schedule of the project, the more benefit an organization will realize from the use of project management. In very basic terms, the organization must allow the project manager to be involved in project initiating and planning. The organization must allow the project manager to influence decision making and to use the project management process to help set realistic expectations.

The value of project management depends on following the complete process from initiating to planning, executing, monitoring and controlling, and closing. However, most executives feel that the process takes too long, and they become impatient. To help address this impatience, project managers must become more effective and efficient in gathering and using data. For those who work in organizations that do not allow the project management process to be followed, data is one of the only ways to show the need for cultural change. Therefore, it is essential for project managers to memorize the type of information that can serve as evidence for the value of good project management practices. For example, a project manager may memorize the last five failed projects in budget and/or schedule, the last five risk items that caused project delay, and the reasons why any quality was compressed. It is also very important for a project manager to understand the entire process of project management and why it exists. When challenged, project managers must educate executives as to why the process exists.

For example, a manager of a project management office (PMO) was very successful in achieving milestone dates and production dates. However, the executives felt that the process to select the dates was too long and wanted faster results. A mandate was passed to select the project date within 60 calendar days from the initiation of the project. But in this organization, it often took between 90 and 120 days to get a contract signed. Therefore, the new mandate forced project managers to select a finish date for the project before a contract defining the work to be completed was finalized.

There are two common types of responses to the mandate used in the example. The first is a quick objection, which sounds like complaining. Executives tend to shun this response and become more resolute in their stance. The second response is general acceptance. This, too, is an ineffective response. If projects begin missing their dates, nobody wins. Instead of either of these two responses, the PMO manager used this as an opportunity to educate and influence. The PMO manager researched the last 30 projects that had been initiated. Then he identified the length of time it took from project initiation to the establishment of the finish date. Within the process, he identified and measured key milestones. The resulting conversation went as follows:

> **PMO Manager:** "I would like to revisit the 60-day rule that you have requested. I completely agree that it seems to take forever for us to pick a

production date. And I absolutely agree a schedule should be established. My team and I are analyzing ways to streamline the process, but we did identify a major constraint."

Executive: "What's that?"

PMO Manager: "Since the team is compensated for hitting milestones and production dates, they want to be sure they do the best possible job of planning. What concerns us is that it takes an average of 97 calendar days to get a contract signed, which means in order to hit the 60 days requested, we would just be making a wild guess at a finish date. Our results would be more accurate if we were to determine a schedule after the contract is signed."

Executive: "I see your point. How about 30 calendar days after the contract signature?"

PMO Manager: "That is more than fair."

This was an actual conversation. There is a perception in many organizations that the process of setting schedules and budgets takes too long. Project managers need to be aware of the perception and work with management to strike a common balance and understanding. It is important to take every opportunity to educate stakeholders about why the process exists. If the process is allowed to occur, there will be a proportional rise in the value of project management.

Unfortunately, most organizations have many more projects than they have the ability to manage. This seems to perpetuate project failure, and consequently, a perceived lack of value in project management. Due to the overwhelming demand for new projects, executives take it upon themselves to establish schedules and budgets and ask the project managers to execute them. Therefore, the next key area to focus on in establishing the value of project management is to address the manner in which projects are selected in the first place.

THE ISSUE WITH PROJECT SELECTION

How are projects selected? What is the process? For many organizations, the selection process is quite arbitrary. It starts with lists of requested projects submitted to management in the form of spreadsheets. Some of the spreadsheets are very basic and some are quite sophisticated, but most indicate the project, the estimated cost, and the potential benefit. These estimates are created at a very high level by the people who desire the projects. Often they are middle managers with little understanding or knowledge of estimation techniques. All of these spreadsheets are then rolled up into another, larger spreadsheet. This activity continues until the total amount requested for the potential projects is calculated. Once the total amount requested is known, a total amount granted then trickles from the top of the organization down. For the most part, this is an unceremonious and painful process that is riddled with the following types of issues:

- **Projects are not selected on their merit.** In most cases, the "squeaky wheel" or the project owner who has the most political influence prevails.

- **Decisions are based on financial considerations only.** Although financial considerations are important, they are not the only consideration that should be included in project selection.

- **Arguments erupt about what was submitted.** During the "roll-up" and "trickle-down" portions of the budgeting process, items on the spreadsheet are adjusted by just about everyone in the process. Often, there are arguments or misunderstandings about which version of the spreadsheet is correct and what number is actually needed.

- **There is no direct link to the organization's strategic plan.** Since the request process starts at a lower level, it is difficult to know which projects support the strategic direction of the organization.

- **Many games are played.** Those who have been through the process learn to manipulate the system to get what they want. This is often at the peril of others in the organization. For instance, a more politically savvy estimator may increase a project estimate to offset what he thinks the potential requested adjustment may be. He may increase the estimate by 20 percent in the hopes that the final budget will only be reduced by 15 percent, thereby preserving what he feels he actually needs for the project.

Each of the previously listed issues is detrimental to an organization. Yet they occur over and over without much change. By following the process described, the company ends up with 175 projects and five project managers to run them. And to top it off, the entire process is based on high-level estimates. The true cost and effort are not known and are rarely asked for when establishing which projects will be selected.

As noted earlier, the spreadsheet will often go through several iterations before becoming finalized. These iterations involve the arbitrary use and manipulation of numbers, such as simply cutting 10 percent of the overall requested amount. Political influence, negotiations, and compromises also come into play. Projects are removed from the list and budgets are reduced in the process of solidifying the list. But this is all done with little consideration or understanding of how each project affects the strategic plan of the company. The ramifications of the removal and reduction of projects and budgets are truly not known and are therefore not understood. There is an old adage that says projects do not fail at completion, they fail at inception. This entire budgeting process lends weight to that statement.

HOW SHOULD PROJECTS BE SELECTED?

The Impact on the Strategic Plan

First and foremost, projects must be selected based on their impact on the organization's overall strategic plan. The most effective way to achieve this is to work from the top down to select projects, and then work from the bottom up to create estimates for those projects. A company should take the agreed-upon strategic plan and break it down like a work breakdown structure (WBS). Not only will this force the understanding of what each strategic initiative means, it will also solidify the path to achieve it. For example, an organization states that its strategic initiative is to revolutionize its presence on the Internet. Most companies' management teams stop at that point and then delegate the "how" to their direct employees. A more thorough and strategic practice would be for the management team to take the next step and identify the projects that will ensure this initiative is met. Essentially, the company should utilize the top-down approach to identify how the organization will meet the initiative. Their breakdown may look like this:

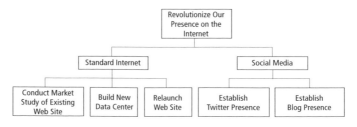

This is then a good transfer point from management to the employees. The next step should be for the rest of the organization to break each project into what needs to happen to achieve the results. Estimates are made at that lower level and then rolled up.

There are two other major considerations that should also be identified for each potential project: business value and capacity.

Business Value

There are several methods that can be utilized to estimate the business value of a project. The method is not as crucial as the documentation of the understanding, however. It is important to clearly convey why the project is necessary and what the true benefits are.

A great example of showing business value comes from a property management company. This company had a process for producing a scorecard for each property. The property managers would fill out a spreadsheet each month consisting of information from various sources and post it on a SharePoint® site. Then an administrator would navigate to each of the 88 SharePoint® sites and create an overall scorecard for the entire company. One of the executives initiated a project to automate this process and show the report as a daily dashboard instead of a monthly report. The cost of the automation was $20,000. On paper, this looked like an easy project to eliminate because there was already a process in place that satisfied the reporting needs. The executive sold his peers on the business value of the project, however: the automated reporting format would rank the property managers every day based on the metrics the company considered important; also, through automation, the potential for manipulation of numbers and the shading of issues that was present with the manual process could be removed. The argument was enough to solidify the selection of the project.

The result of the project was even more staggering than anticipated. The project had a payback period of 36 hours. When the first rankings came out, suffice it to say it was not a good thing to be ranked dead last. This instituted a frenzy of activity to improve the rankings. One of the biggest jumps could be made by eliminating any balance in the bad debt column. Roughly $160,000 was collected on the first day the rankings were released. This was money that the company was about to write off. Therefore, this project created an 800 percent return on investment in 36 hours and placed the most important metrics and performance information in front of the entire company every day. The business value was much more significant than just the financial cost of the project itself. If cost had been the only criteria considered, this project would have never been approved.

Capacity
The interest in portfolio management has been increasing lately in the business community, as many companies

are trying to understand their organization's capacity to do projects. There is a type of capacity that is often overlooked, however—the capacity to perform project management on those projects.

The best way to determine project management capacity is to first establish three or four tiers to use in classifying projects. Tier 1 should include the most strategic projects or the projects with the most risk. Tier 2 should include highly strategic projects that are shorter in duration or are not as risky. Tier 3 should include single unit or department initiatives. Finally, tier 4 should include internal initiatives or projects that can be run by team leads. Based on the governance models of the organization, the company should assign an estimate of a percentage of a project manager's time to each tier. For instance, a typical tier 1 project may take up 50 percent of a project manager's time, whereas a tier 2 project may be expected to only take up 35 percent. Once the tiers and estimates have been established, the project management capacity can be determined. For example:

If tier 1 = 50%, tier 2 = 35%, tier 3 = 15%, and the company has 5 project managers, then the company's total project management capacity could be:

10 tier 1 projects (500%); or 5 tier 1 projects (250%) + 5 tier 2 projects (175%) + 5 tier 3 projects (75%); or any combination that equals 500%.

This method determines an organization's real project management capacity and creates a much different result than the norm of 175 projects for 5 project managers.

Once strategic value, financial considerations, business value, and capacity are understood, the organization can make the decisions of which projects are accepted and which are not. This is not done by the normal process of arbitrarily cutting projects and reducing budgets. Instead, the organization should use the information gathered to reevaluate the overall strategic plan. For instance, if it appears that three more project managers will be needed to complete the entire strategic plan, the organization needs to decide to either get three more project managers or to reduce the outcome of a particular strategic objective and remove the projects that would have required the additional project managers. Since all of the projects were created from the top down, then all of the projects are tied to strategic initiatives. The removal or reduction of a strategic initiative will remove or reduce the projects needed to meet that initiative.

The approach promoted in this chapter will only work if the executives embrace the process of project management and work with their project managers to do a better job of project initiation and selection. Once the process has been embraced, the value of project management will truly be felt and much less difficult to articulate.

Now that we've looked at the current status of the profession and how to articulate the value of project management, it is time to find out how to stop playing the games that consistently devalue the profession of project management.

3 | The Pricing Game

The best we can do is size up the chances, calculate the risks involved, estimate our ability to deal with them, and then make our plans with confidence.

> – Henry Ford, American industrialist and pioneer of the assembly-line production method

The greatest of all gifts is the power to estimate things at their true worth.

> – François de La Rochefoucauld, French classical author

The pricing game can be one of the most frustrating and time-consuming activities for a project manager. As a project manager, you are often asked to select a number out of thin air. Even though you are told that the number will only be used to set expectations, it frequently becomes the budgeted number. The types of experiences you have had, or the culture of your organization, will determine how big of a guess it becomes. For many project managers, it is as if they have been placed on a game show where they have just seen some fabulous prizes and they have to guess how much the prize package costs. Of course, there are rules and stipulations to guessing the price in order to win. The interesting thing is that most of the time, the project managers are completely unaware of those rules. Here is how the conversation generally goes:

> **Executive:** "We have budgets due tomorrow, and I want to include a figure for that new technology we discussed. Do you have an idea of the cost?"

> **PM:** "I have no idea what it would cost. There are several avenues that we could go down."

> **Executive:** "Just give me a number so I can get budget approval. I won't hold you to it."

> **PM:** "I am not sure; maybe $500,000?"

> **Executive:** "I know I won't be able to get that much. How about $200,000?"

> **PM:** "I guess that would work."

> **Executive:** "Great."

Now we fast-forward to the end of planning and the beginning of the execution of the project:

> **PM:** "OK, to deliver this new technology, the cost is going to be $425,000."

> **Executive:** "What? We only have $200,000 budgeted! You need to deliver this project for $200,000."

Unfortunately, this is not an oversimplification of this conversation. Project managers are frequently asked for a "budgetary" figure that they "will not be held to." The number thrown as the budgetary figure then becomes the budget and turns into a constraint on the project. This practice is what leads many project managers to pad their estimates.

COMING IN UNDER BUDGET CAN BE JUST AS BAD!

There are many organizations in which it is common practice to pad estimates to the point that it becomes detrimental to the organization. It seems the goal of the budgeting process is often to protect what the estimator wants at the expense of the overall needs of the organization. Here is an actual statement from a division manager of a Fortune 50 company:

> **Division Manager:** "I am so excited! I needed $2 million for all of my projects. I asked for $3.5 million and got $2.2 million. I have $200,000 to play with this year!"

This type of behavior and culture is detrimental to an organization. Think of all of the projects that did not get selected because of budget shortfalls, or the divisions that do not have the political influence to get everything they need. These pricing games are played in almost every organization. Such games are born out of mistrust, misinformation, and the unwillingness to be honest. They are especially prevalent in organizations that have a lack of visibility and accountability into the work that is being completed.

Pricing games are played when executives, middle management, and team members are not completely honest with each other. So what can be done to fix this? How about changing the rules of the game? Organizations should develop a reward system or initiative so that people "win" the game by becoming as efficient as possible, estimating the price as closely as possible to the end cost without going over. The divisions that achieve such estimates should then be rewarded by getting budget increases, not shortfalls.

How can organizations track the divisions that should "win"? By applying all of the metrics that are defined throughout this chapter. Tracking these metrics will identify the groups that are doing the best jobs of estimating and those that are trying to play the game.

In Rita Mulcahy's *PMP® Exam Prep* book, she offers keen insights and tips to project managers. One of the tips that project managers have a tough time accepting states that "Padding is a sign of poor project management!" When this is said in a classroom setting, a student or two will comment, "She has never worked for my company," or "I have to pad; it is the only way to get what I need."

Padding *is* a sign of poor project management. As noted earlier, people may pad their numbers because they expect management to cut a percentage off their estimates. But project managers also pad if they don't trust their own estimates. They use the pad as a buffer for protection. And management knows padding is happening. Thus, we have the pricing game. This game must stop. It creates mistrust with stakeholders, and it devalues the profession of project management.

You may feel that even though you do not want to throw a number, pad an estimate, or guess, you are often forced to do so. But even when forced, you can begin to establish context and utilize project management tools like PERT instead of playing the pricing game.

HOW TO UTILIZE PERT

It is important to understand that the best way to create an estimate is to follow the principles of project management. This involves creating a WBS with the help of the team, identifying work packages, receiving estimates from the team for cost and effort, completing a thorough risk analysis, establishing a contingency plan and reserve, and gaining buy-in from stakeholders. Unfortunately, many executives will routinely bypass this whole process and state, "Just throw me a number."

Using PERT (Program Evaluation and Review Technique) is an alternative to playing the pricing game.

PERT is one of the most important tools to establish context for your estimates. The formula for PERT is:

ESTIMATE

[Best Case + (4 × Most Likely) + Worst Case] / 6

This formula utilizes a three-point estimate and a standard distribution curve to create a much more realistic estimate than pulling a number out of the air. You can stop here, or for budgeting purposes, you can go one step further to determine what the variance of the estimate will be. This is calculated with the following formula:

VARIABLE

(Worst Case – Best Case) / 6

Now let's put this formula into action. Assume you are asked to estimate a project with little definition. Using your expert opinion, you quickly estimate that:

Best Case = $200,000

Most Likely = $400,000

Worst Case = $500,000

PERT Calculation = [$200,000 + (4 × $400,000) + $500,000] / 6

PERT Number = $383,333

Variance Calculation = ($500,000 – $200,000) / 6

Variance Number = $50,000

Therefore, the project estimate is
$383,333 +/- $50,000.

There are generally three groups of project managers when it comes to PERT. There are those who utilize it successfully, those who have never heard of it, and those who just memorized the formula to become certified project managers. What can be frustrating for many holding the Project Management Professional (PMP®) certification is that they were told to memorize certain formulas or tools, but they were never taught why or how to use them. If your eyes have glazed over at this point or you feel that you will never have an opportunity to actually use this formula, this is the time to really pay attention.

It is understood that in the real world, you may not have time to calculate PERT, or you may have very little information from which to make an estimate. The key of this formula and the intent of its use are to truly establish context. In other words, introduce doubt. Project managers can use PERT to help their sponsors understand that estimates are very wide-ranging on a project and cannot be refined until more is known about the scope of the project. The sponsors can then use the provided range to help them make a decision on a budget amount without forcing the project manager to make an uneducated guess.

One of the biggest misconceptions in project management is that the responsibility for deciding what to do in times of turmoil rests on the project manager. So if the project has exceeded budget or schedule, the project manager must decide how to fix it. This is not the case, however. The job of the project manager is to assess the impact of the information, present options to the sponsors and stakeholders, and then execute upon the direction given.

Now, if a project manager applies the concept of PERT and understands that his or her role is to present accurate information and options about the project to the sponsor and stakeholders, the conversation we used earlier becomes radically different. Let's look at the following two cases:

Case 1

A project manager is walking down the hallway and has been stopped by a sponsor. The project manager does not have time to run the actual PERT calculations.

> **Executive:** "We have budgets due tomorrow, and I want to include a figure for that new technology we discussed. Do you have an idea of the cost?"

PM: "Based on the limited information that I have, I think in the best case it could be as low as $200,000 but it could also be as much as $500,000. I would need more time and information to come up with an exact figure."

Executive: "Just give me a number so I can get budget approval. I won't hold you to it."

PM: "If I had to pick a number right now, to be safe we may need to go with the worst case."

Executive: "I know I won't be able to get that much. How about $200,000?"

PM: "That is the best case option. I can't promise we would be able to do it for that. Without time to plan, it is the highest risk to choose that number. But in the end, it is really your call."

Executive: "Great."

In this case, the project manager established a range of estimates showing uncertainty about the total cost. The estimates were not padded. The project manager simply created a reasonable range and presented the options to the sponsor. The sponsor now has the information to make the best decision possible and is responsible for that decision. Yes, the sponsor may still push for the best-case number. In this case, the following conversation might occur in the future meeting when the final numbers are determined:

> **PM:** "OK, to deliver this new technology, the cost is going to be $425,000."

> **Executive:** "What? We only have $200,000 budgeted! You need to deliver this project for $200,000."

> **PM:** "I stated that this project could cost up to $500,000 and that $200,000 would be the best-case and riskiest number. Now that we truly know all of the information, the cost is $425,000. But we have some options. We can reduce scope, try to bid it out, or not do the project. What would you like to do?"

You may scoff at this scenario and say it could not be done in your environment. Some organizational cultures don't encourage such frank conversations. By using the best-case and worst-case estimates in the initial conversation, however, you can set up the opportunity to have the conversation. It is important to establish the context of how you estimated the information. In this case, the project manager established a reasonable range of estimates and gave the disclaimer that more information would be needed to come up with a better number. The decision of which estimate to use was then in the sponsor's hands.

Case 2

A project manager receives a request for an estimate for new technology in an e-mail. Since the request was sent via e-mail, the project manager has time to provide all of the PERT numbers. Here is the e-mail response:

Sponsor,

Based on the limited information that we have, the range of the estimate needs to be between $200,000 and $500,000. If we have to pick a number to go with, the best estimate I can offer is roughly $380,000, plus or minus $50,000.

Project Manager

In this case, the project manager presented the best case and worst case, selected the PERT number, and gave the sponsor the variance of the estimate. Most likely, the sponsor will use the information provided to select a number within the range. However, if the sponsor presses the issue further, the project manager can answer, "Based on the information we have at this time, I estimate $380,000, but I could be off by as much as $50,000 either way." The project manager is answering the question with realistic options. Now let's see how the later conversation might go in this case:

PM: "OK, to deliver this new technology, the cost is going to be $425,000."

Executive: "What? We only have $200,000 budgeted! You need to deliver this project for $200,000."

PM: "The number I estimated was $380,000, and we were off by less than the $50,000 anticipated. $425,000 is what it will cost. What would you like to do?"

It is very likely that in either of the cases presented, the sponsor will still insist that the project manager has to do the project for $200,000. In that situation, the culture change will occur when the organization has to answer the question, "Why did this project fail?" Over time, the sponsor will begin to understand the value of the project manager's estimates and the culture change will begin. And once this shift has started through a broad understanding of estimating, organizations can continue to increase the accuracy of their estimates by using risk management and risk information.

USE RISK MANAGEMENT AND RISK INFORMATION

Risk is truly a misunderstood concept. Project managers flock to seminars and books about how to do risk management and maintain risk information, yet they fail to apply any of the concepts to their real-world projects. Risk is hard. It is an advanced topic. But the approach of using risk management and risk information in the context of estimates is as simple as documentation and

memorization. For every estimate that is given, the
following metrics need to be recorded:

Initial Estimates	
Date Estimate Requested *The date the sponsor requested the estimate*	
Best-Case Estimate *Your best-case estimate*	
Most Likely Estimate *Your most likely estimate*	
Worst-Case Estimate *Your worst-case estimate*	
PERT Estimate *Formula: (Best Case + (4 × Most Likely) + Worst Case) / 6*	
Estimate Variance *Formula: (Worst Case – Best Case) / 6*	
Budget Number Selected by Sponsor *The figure that actually made it into the budget*	
Planning	
Date Project Started Planning *The date planning on the project started*	
Estimate Presented by Project Manager *The figure you requested after planning*	

Planning (Continued)	
Date Estimate Presented by Project Manager *The date you presented the refined figure*	
Baseline Estimate *The figure that was in the sanctioned budget*	
Project Completion	
Actual Cost *The actual cost of the project*	

It may be difficult to get all of these metrics if there are multiple project managers involved, but you should try to get as many of these as possible. If you are a part of a project management office (PMO), these metrics need to be added to the systems or spreadsheets that you use. With these metrics in place, the following can be determined:

- **Actual Cost vs. Baseline Estimate** (the most commonly tracked financial metric)

- **Actual Cost vs. Estimate Presented by the Project Manager** (the most commonly forgotten metric)

- **Actual Cost vs. PERT Estimate**

- **Estimate Presented by the Project Manager vs. Baseline Estimate**

- **Time Elapsed between Date Estimate Requested and Date Estimate Presented by Project Manager**

Once the metrics are recorded, you should memorize the average numbers. This will allow you to have the most information possible for those hallway conversations. Applying the concept of using data, let's revisit the hallway conversation presented earlier:

> **Executive:** "We have budgets due tomorrow, and I want to include a figure for that new technology we discussed. Do you have an idea of the cost?"

> **PM:** "Based on the limited information that I have, I think in the best case it could be as low as $200,000 but it could also be as much as $500,000. I would need more time and information to come up with an exact figure."

> **Executive:** "Just give me a number so I can get budget approval. I won't hold you to it."

> **PM:** "If I had to pick a number right now, to be safe we may need to go with the worst case."

> **Executive:** "I know I won't be able to get that much. How about $200,000?"

> **PM:** "That could be really risky. For the last ten projects in which we selected the best-case estimate, only one out of the ten actually hit that number. Eight out of the last ten hit just below our most likely estimate. To be safe, we should use

PERT to calculate the estimate. Would you mind if
I e-mailed that to you when I am back at my desk?"

Executive: "Great."

Simply knowing the statistics can make a profound
difference in setting the context of an estimate. If you win
the battle of context, you will see the success statistics of
your project implementations skyrocket.

NEVER JUST THROW A NUMBER

Hopefully, you have now been convinced that
just "throwing a number" is not conducive to the
organization or to the practice of project management.
As discussed in chapter 1, it is recognized that
professionals like accountants and actuaries must execute
a process in order to determine an outcome. Project
managers are certified and trained to do the same thing.
However, project managers are routinely asked to "just
throw a number."

One of the best defenses to a request to "throw a
number" is to provide an answer that is just as a
ridiculous as the request. For example, a consultant is
meeting with an executive team about the establishment
of a PMO. The question posed by an executive is, "How
much will it cost to establish a PMO?" The consultant has
only been meeting with them for about 30 minutes and
cannot possibly answer that question with any degree of

accuracy. Therefore, he uses the defense of humor. The conversation goes as follows:

Executive: "How much will it cost to implement a PMO?"

PM: "That is difficult to say since there are a tremendous number of variables."

Executive: "Just throw a number for a budgetary figure. We won't hold you to it."

PM: (jokingly) "Since you won't hold me to it, I think it is more than safe to say that I guarantee it will cost less than $5 million."

Executive: "Wow...that is a big number!"

PM: "In all seriousness, I have no idea what the cost would be to implement here, but let's continue our conversation and once I understand everything you want, I can guide you to what you need. There are many options out there; it all depends on what it will take to make your team successful."

Utilizing humor can be a great defense in having to throw a number. Regardless of the circumstances, motivations, or reasons, never just throw a number. You will be held to it and you will be constrained by it. It should not be difficult to ask for even an hour to come up with something usable. It is important to make sure that context is established at every step of the process. Utilizing PERT, setting the appropriate context for pricing conversations, and using traceable metrics are ways to stop the pricing game. Getting to the data, tracking the metrics, and having more honest conversations with your sponsor will help you gain confidence as a project manager. The approach presented in this chapter will begin to build a new relationship with your sponsor and allow you to continue to introduce project management best practices to the organization.

4 Guess the Truth!

You can bend it and twist it...you can misuse it and abuse it... but even God can't change the truth.

– Michael Levy

Man is least himself when he talks in his own person. Give him a mask, and he will tell you the truth.

– Oscar Wilde, Irish Poet, Novelist, Dramatist, and Critic

Project managers can be some of the most optimistic and hopeful people in the world. They hope that another month is going to generate out of thin air, or they hope that they will trip over a huge bag of cash on the way to work. When such things do not occur, they really begin to panic! Several studies report that inexperienced project managers are a key reason projects fail. Project failures do not always occur at the technical level; instead, failure may occur at the communication level. Many inexperienced project managers seem to be afraid to reveal what is really happening on the project because they feel it is a poor reflection of their skills.

They are reluctant to reveal the truth. They gloss over the facts in the status report and will not report that the project is behind schedule or over budget. Their hope is that somehow the project will get back on track or that money will fall out of the sky before they have to reveal what is really going on. Of course, when those things do not occur, many times it is too late to really do something about it. Project managers must learn that, although a poor schedule, budget, or process can reflect poorly on them, it is not as bad as withheld information. The truth really can set you free.

IT IS WHAT IT IS!

"It is what it is" should become the mantra of project managers. Any time they are faced with a difficult situation, poor result, or bad news, it is what it is. No amount of hope, spin, prayer, or positive thinking can change the current facts of the project. When projects are going well, project managers are unafraid to tell the world of the progress. It is when things are not going well that you can truly find out what type of project manager you are. Will you be bold and tell the truth, or will you accentuate the positives while trying to ignore the negatives? Eventually the actual progress will come out. When it does, will you be able to be resolute knowing that you have been truthful in your reports?

There are normally a few reasons project managers are not truthful or do not give the entire picture when reporting status:

- They are hopeful that the project will make up time or budget before they have to reveal the truth.
- Cultural pressures make them gloss over the truth (e.g., a manager tells them to change a status).
- They fear the true project status will have ramifications against their employment.
- They do not know the actual status of the project.

These issues each carry their own challenge, but they are mostly related to fear. Fear of the unknown. Fear of the reaction of management. Fear that the project manager will lose his or her job if others find out the project is not going well.

This lack of truthfulness leads to a lack of trust. And if the executives, team members, or peers do not trust the project manager, then the project has an extremely high risk of failure. For those who have not told the entire truth, or have simply lied about the current status of the project, when the truth does come out, it is devastating. To be successful in project management, project managers must operate in a trustworthy fashion.

There is a freedom that comes with adopting an attitude of "it is what it is." For example, if a project manager is on a project that is way behind schedule, the sooner the true status is revealed, the more options to correct the situation are available. Don't believe that statement? Ask yourself, what are the most common activities cut or reduced out of a project? Overwhelmingly, the answer is testing, training, or quality, depending on the type of project. So what is the reason for these activities being cut? Simple—these are the last things that are done on a project. For instance, in a software development project, if the development falls behind, then the code is released to the testers late. If the date is a mandated date and can't be moved, the only thing left to compress is testing. This is where executives or sponsors will look at a project plan and say, "We know we planned for eight weeks of testing, but we will just put eight people on it and do it in a week!" The reason testing, training, or quality activities are reduced is that the hope that time will be made up has run out. Since the project manager did not reveal where the project really was, the only thing left to do is to covertly degrade quality.

However, in the "it is what it is" world, the status of the project is revealed earlier, when there are more options available to bring the project back on track. Let's look at the following example:

- Project Manager A is aware that the project is behind in the third month of a six-month development project. Every week the project manager meets with the developers and hopes that they will make up time, and every week they get a bit more behind. When the developers are actually done, there is only one month of project time left. The plan called for two months of testing and training before rollout. The project manager now switches the hope of making up time to the hope that there is really nothing found in the testing of the product. The decision is made by the project manager to reduce testing. But bugs are found. Now the decision is to implement workarounds or quick fixes that will be "permanently fixed at a later time." The project comes in on schedule, but the quality is greatly reduced. At this point in the project, the project manager switches to hoping the executives do not discover what really happened.

- Project Manager B adopts an "it is what it is" attitude. As soon as the project is behind, the project manager reports it. The difference is that the difficulty is known in the third month of the project. The options available are to reduce the scope, add resources, or absorb the delay. The project manager is dealing with the issue versus hoping that the issue goes away. Even if management becomes upset, it is temporary, since there are options to fix the issue.

And if management does become upset, would you rather be Project Manager A or B?

A further example looks at a project manager on a technology deployment project. He announces that they are 55 hours behind schedule on the third week of a nine-month effort. The conversation goes as follows:

Client: "I see on your status report that you are reporting a 55-hour overage on the third week of a nine-month project! How is this even possible?"

PM: "I can understand your concern. One of the risks we had identified on the project was the readiness of the warehouse. The team had to do some additional work when this risk occurred, and it has put us behind schedule."

Client: "We can't move the date. How are you going to make up the time?"

PM: "That is a great question. Right now, our mitigation plan is to see how the next three weeks go. We want to get the process started and see if we can find some efficiencies that will speed up the process. My goal is to report how that is going in each status report. If at the end of three weeks we have not made up significant time, would it be acceptable to bring some options to you on how to ensure the requested date?"

Client: "Sure. I will be watching."

The "it is what it is" attitude does not have to be negative, forceful, or combative. It is simply a truthful delivery of the status. The project manager has established several things with the client. First and foremost, credibility. The client immediately gets the impression that the project manager is in control of the project. The second thing is that the project manager will be protecting the date the client had requested. The third thing is that the project manager will be providing options should the project not get back on track. Many project managers underestimate the power of simply revealing the truth.

FORCE THE DECISION—ASK FOR WHAT YOU NEED!

Revealing the truth is only half of the battle. This is what the project managers who have revealed the truth only to have it blow up in their faces have failed to recognize. It is not just the truth that is needed, but options to deal with the truth as well. You must provide both the current status of the project and options to rebalance the project if necessary. PMI® teaches that when the actual performance of a project deviates from the established baseline, the project manager must analyze the deviation and create options to bring the project back in line. This is the theory of preventive and corrective actions.

Preventive actions are taken to prevent a project from deviating from the project baseline. These are generally smaller items completely within the control of the project manager to enact. The actions are identified through processes like risk management and quality assurance and are part of the quality management effort. In Six Sigma, a very popular quality methodology, there are what are known as defects. Defects are any process outputs that either do not meet the customer specifications or that could lead to an output that does not meet customer specifications. When a defect is found and corrected prior to it impacting the customer, it is no longer a defect. Preventive actions work in the same way. If the scope, budget, or schedule begins to slide and the project manager enacts a preventive action, then the deviation is no longer an issue.

Corrective actions are a bit harder to enact and are the types of actions that project managers should disclose. Corrective actions are handled according to the project's change management plan. This is an area where many project managers go astray. Somewhere along the way during the evolution of their careers, many project managers have come to assume that they must make the decision about how to bring a project back on track. But it is not their decision to make! On most projects, change control is not in the power of the project manager. Instead, as identified in the change management plan, the sponsors and stakeholders are responsible for such decisions. However, when a project manager covertly takes an action that degrades quality, the project manager is taking the decision upon him- or herself. In essence, this allows executives to have plausible deniability. By not taking the decision to the executives, for better or worse, the project manager has put the fate of the entire project on his or her shoulders.

There are many project managers out there who are unable to sleep at night due to the stress and worry of carrying such burdens. What seems to be lost is the understanding that it is not the project manager's position to make the decision! Instead, the project manager's job is to measure performance, identify deviations, and if deviations occur, analyze the impact to the overall project plan and present options.

What is interesting is that when project managers bring options to executives, they may find that things are not as "set in stone" as they had believed. For example, a project manager was implementing a large solution. Contractually, the completion date was to be March 31. When the project manager created the project plan, however, the earliest completion date, based on all of the constraints, was April 25. The entire project team was in a panic and was asking the project manager what to do. Many project managers who bear such burdens would not publish the real date of April 25, but would instead succumb to the pressure of March 31 and try to do everything possible to make the date. But this project manager, who believed in "it is what it is," presented the information to the sponsor. The sponsor, upon hearing the date of April 25, felt that it was an acceptable date and allowed the plan to be baselined in its current state. That was it—no additional work was necessary. By the project manager presenting the facts as known, the executive could make a decision, and in this case, it worked out to the benefit of the team.

If in reading that last example you just said to yourself, "That will never work in my company," you might be right. But what if you are wrong? Have you ever tried to present an alternative date? Have you ever asked for the reasoning behind the selected date and budget? Do you assume that the date or budget is mandated, or do you *know* that it is mandated? Even in the previous example, if the sponsor said that March 31 was an absolute, at least now the situation is understood. Do you have a fear of presenting such information to your sponsor? If the date is likely to be missed, accepting the date anyway and hoping it is not missed is a guarantee of failure. Presenting the sponsor with alternatives and then forcing the sponsor to make a decision may not turn out in your favor. But you are more likely to succeed if you at least try.

MAKE ASSUMPTIVE STATEMENTS

Many times project managers who have tried to ask for what they need still have not received it. The reason for this is often in how they ask the question. In project management, the technique of assumptive statements can be highly useful. Do not ask yes or no questions; instead, ask either/or questions. The latter format at least forces a conversation.

Here is an example. A project manager has received a mandated date of June 30. After working with the team and completing the project management planning process, the project manager determines that the expected completion date is October 15. The project manager begins to utilize techniques like crashing and fast tracking to see how the project timeline can be improved. The answer is that five more resources are necessary. The project manager feels that the executive will not allow the additional resources. Now let's look at the different ways to address the question:

Yes/No Format

> **PM:** "Can I have five more resources for this project?"

> **Executive:** "We don't have five resources available."

This pretty much ends the conversation. Since it was posed as a yes or no type of question, once the answer is received, there is not much else to say. Now for the other option:

Either/Or Format

> **PM:** "In order to hit the date requested, we need five more resources, or the date will be October 15."

> **Executive:** "We don't have five resources available."

PM: "Then we're looking at an end date of October 15."

By stating that the company did not have five additional resources, the executive was by default selecting the later date. Even if the executive becomes combative, the project manager is still in a great position:

Either/Or Format

PM: "In order to hit the date requested, we need five more resources or the date will be October 15."

Executive: "We don't have five resources available."

PM: "Then we're looking at an end date of October 15."

Executive: "Absolutely not! The finish date will be June 30 as stated!"

PM: "Okay. But then we're back to the question of resources. Do you have any ideas about how we will find the resources to achieve that date?

Executive: "You will not be able to find those resources; we do not have them."

PM: "According to our project plan, we would need the resources to ensure the date. Since it's clear that we do not have the resources, do you want to look at reducing the scope or extending the date?"

(In these types of situations, if executives revert back to one of their favorite sayings, they are still responsible for the outcome.)

Executive: "Just make it happen."

PM: "I apologize sir, but make what happen?"

Executive: "Do whatever it takes to get the project in by June 30."

PM: "So, do you want me to reduce the scope or find alternative resources?"

This conversation can go round and round and on and on. But if the project manager had not even approached the executive with the information, the project would have automatically been doomed. And even if the executive cuts off the conversation at "Just make it happen," the point for the project manager has been made. Although the executive did not make a decision, the fact that the project manager presented the options will change a future conversation. That future conversation will likely begin with, "Why did this project fail?" By making assumptive statements, the project manager asked for what was needed and therefore can be free of the worry, guilt, or panic that he or she may have otherwise felt.

There is one very key item to avoid in these conversations. Do not press too hard. Clearly present the options, accept the answer given, and then document the results. Pressing too hard could damage the relationship with the executive. If you document the options and response, then you will have that documentation to refer to in the lessons learned session. Over time, the executive will begin to realize that certain mandates have consequences. This may take days, weeks, months, or even years, but the change will occur. Making assumptive statements forces the decision back to the sponsors where it belongs.

DON'T THROW IT IF YOU DON'T KNOW IT!

One of the most important items in making assumptive statements and forcing the decisions needed is to ensure you have the data. Make sure you follow the principles of project management and complete the planning processes. You must have the data to support the assumptive statements used in this chapter. If you throw a number or a consequence out and do not have the data to support it, then your credibility will be severely damaged. Do not give information that you have not researched or you are not reasonably certain is correct.

There are three words that seem to be neglected by many project managers: "I don't know." Say it aloud: "I don't know." That wasn't that scary, was it? An even better phrase is, "Can I get back to you with that?" If you are uncertain of the answer to the question, the impact to the plan, or the outcome of the decision, it is much better to get back to the requestor with the real information than guess and give them wrong information. It is perfectly acceptable to not know every answer to every question. Do not feel pressured to have to make something up. Even if the requestor is demanding the information, you can qualify it by saying, "I am not 100 percent sure, but..." or "I believe this is true, but can I get back to you after I validate the information I am using?"

If you don't know it, don't throw it. It is a sure way to allow the games played around projects to happen, and then everyone loses. It is time for project managers to stop playing the games that cause project failure.

5 | Grapevine

Many attempts to communicate are nullified by saying too much.

– Robert Greenleaf

Sometimes there is a greater lack of communication in facile talking than in silence.

– Faith Baldwin

A phenomenon on projects is that people will create "grapevine" communications in the absence of official communications. The exponential communication paths grow and grow, and the more there are, the more complex the network becomes. If you, as the project manager, are not sending official communications, then the grapevine communications become the official ones. In fact, people tend to communicate more when there is a lack of formal project communication. These communications are generally ill-informed and can be inaccurate. The information also tends to be interpreted and changed as it passes from person to person on the project.

If you ever played the grapevine game as a child, you understand the phenomenon. In the movie *Johnny Dangerously* (Twentieth Century Fox Film Corporation, 1984), the main character is in jail. Someone wants to send him a message through the jail grapevine. The message starts as, "Vermin is going to kill Johnny's brother at the Savoy Theater. Pass it on." The message gets sent through the grapevine until the final exchange:

Prisoner: "There's a message through the grapevine, Johnny."

Johnny Dangerously: "Yeah? What is it?"

Prisoner: "Johnny and the Mothers are playing 'Stompin' at the Savoy in Vermont tonight."

Johnny Dangerously: "Vermin's going to kill my brother at the Savoy Theater tonight!"

Prisoner: "I didn't say that."

Johnny Dangerously: "No, but I know this grapevine!"

As in the movie, the project grapevine actually becomes a game of password. Participants must guess at several clues in order to get the correct information. It is up to the project manager to ensure this does not become the case.

COMMUNICATE OFTEN

Projects succeed or fail based on the context of the message. Therefore, the project manager must control communications on a project. Really controlling the flow of the information needs to go beyond the traditional communications. Many project managers rely on status reports to tell the story, but status reports are simply content; they rarely show the context of the information. This is an age-old problem that project teams have been trying to solve since the inception of project teams. Why do you think there are so many different methodologies and systems to relay project status? Let's look at some of the most popular methods.

Standard Status Report

The standard status report is generally a stoplight approach showing red, yellow, or green as the status. There are issues with this type of report, however. First, it is usually subjective. Second, the indirect path that status reports typically take through an organization can present opportunities for interference with the report. For instance, some companies have serious integrity issues when it comes to status reports. There are many stories in which a project manager reports something one way and the middle manager changes the status before it is sent to higher managers. Here is an example.

In one company, a consultant was hired to assist with the organization's project management maturity. After a few weeks, the consultant found out that his progress reports, which showed red, were being changed to green and then passed to the executives by a middle manager. When the consultant met with the team, they reported similar stories and were very frustrated. The consultant adopted an "it is what it is" approach and started being more detailed in his reports. The middle manager continued to change the reports and was completely unaware that the consultant and project team knew of his behavior. The consultant asked the middle manager if his reports were being edited, and the middle manager said they were not. In this organization, the consultant had no other recourse but to let the events play out.

Eventually, the project failed. The consultant was called into the executive's office to explain the failure. The consultant knew that the culture of the organization did not favor him calling the middle manager out. Therefore, the consultant had to choose his words wisely. The conversation went as follows:

> **Executive:** "Why did this project fail? We hired you to prevent these things from happening!"

> **Consultant:** "I apologize, but I am a bit confused."

> **Executive:** "What is there to be confused about? We hired you to do a job and you failed!"

Consultant: "I guess what I am confused about is that it sounds like this is the first time that you understood the project was failing."

Executive: "Well of course it is!"

Consultant: "That is where I am confused. I have been reporting this project was in trouble for the last four months and have been asking for assistance."

Executive: "I never heard that. How were you asking for assistance? How were you reporting the project was in trouble?"

Consultant: "In my status reports, sir. My status reports have shown red for four months with several issues."

Executive: "I have seen nothing but green on the reports given to me."

Consultant: "Hmm. I am not sure how that happened. The reports I sent to the middle manager showed as all red. I guess we could check with him."

The rest of the story is history. It became evident that the middle manager was causing a lot of the issues, and he was eventually removed.

Another organization asked a project management consultant to automate their status reports. The company was very proud of the format and the information contained in the report. However, it took a manual effort of 1,000 total hours per month to pull together the status report. As a result, it was released two to three weeks after the end of the month. Essentially, the information could be six or seven weeks old by the time it was reported. The effort and timeline involved made a great case for automation, but it also raised other concerns. The consultant asked some key questions: "When was the last time you made a real decision off of this report? Meaning, when was the last time you saw something as yellow and you devoted resources or funds to turn it back to green? When was the last time you stopped a project because it was red too long? What were the last three key decisions made because of this report?" No one in the organization could answer. So many times, reports are generated for unknown reasons or without a basis for outcome. Companies need to make sure that they receive value from the reports, not just a bunch of colors.

And speaking of colors, here is yet another example of issues encountered. The PMO manager in an organization wanted to change the status report colors from red, yellow, and green to what the PMO manager felt was a more internationally friendly version. The organization had invested in an Internet-based project and portfolio management tool, and the PMO manager now wanted to change the red to a storm cloud, the yellow to partly sunny, and the green to a full sun. The PMO manager felt that the stoplight system was not internationally recognizable because some countries do not have stoplights. He thought the weather icons would be easier to understand. The consultant who was working with the organization questioned the value of such a change, however, and suggested that if a country did not have a stoplight, people in that country most likely would not be firing up a computer to look at an Internet-based project management system to find the status of a project. Suffice it to say, there can be quite a few problems and misconceptions with status reports—some more serious than others, of course.

Percent Complete

Another popular way to report the status of a project is to use a percent complete model. This includes one of the absolute worst questions that a project manager can ask: "What percent complete are you?" The person who is asked this question will step back, do some quick mental calculations, and then say something like, "40 percent." But what they really did in their head was to say, "Oh no, I haven't started yet. However, I think I can be 80 percent complete the next time she asks me, so I am going to lie and say 40 percent." All of the subjective answers then roll up to an overall percentage. This is how a project becomes 95 percent complete after the first three months and 96 percent complete three months later.

Earned Value

This is by far one of the most complex systems for reporting status. It was born out of the fact that when a project manager shows a percent complete, there is not enough context to tell if the project is ahead or behind schedule or budget. This system uses the cost and schedule baselines, and compares actual hours and cost against planned work and cost. The system is much more reliable than other methods of reporting status; however, it can be very difficult if the organization does not do a great job of creating work breakdown structures and overall planning. To be successful, the project must have estimated durations, estimated effort, and a regular feedback system to receive the actual percentage of work completed, the actual cost, and the actual effort expended. Since many project managers can rarely determine the total amount of effort that will be involved in their projects, earned value is nearly impossible.

So if these popular methods of reporting status all have issues, what should you do? As noted in the next section, one thing you can do is change your methods of communication.

CHANGE YOUR METHODS OF COMMUNICATION

To truly succeed in managing projects, you must change your methods of communication. You can still use many of the same formats to report the status of the project, but you need to ask questions in a slightly different manner.

For instance, instead of asking, "What percent complete are you?" the question should be stated as, "How much time have you spent on this activity, and how much time do you have remaining?" With this information, you are still able to report a percent complete, but asking for it this way requires more accountability from the resource.

Let's look at an example where this concept was applied. A project manager had a virtual resource designing a data warehouse. The project manager was unsure of how the work was progressing. The conversation went as follows:

> **PM:** "What percent complete are you on the design of the warehouse?"

> **Resource:** "Um...35 percent complete."

> **PM:** "Let me ask that a different way. How many hours have you worked on this activity, and how many hours do you think you have remaining?"

> **Resource:** "I know I have worked 55 hours on the activity. I am not sure how many I have remaining. Maybe another 100?"

> **PM:** "55 hours. Great. Can you show me?"

> **Resource:** "Show you what?"

> **PM:** "What does 55 hours buy me?"

Resource: "Uh...um...I really don't have anything to show you."

PM: "55 hours of design and you have nothing to show? No document, no drawings, no notes on the back of a napkin?"

Resource: "No."

The resource had been taking advantage of the remote situation. The project manager's adjustment of the way he asked for status accomplished two things. First, it got him a quantitative response (55 hours) that was easier to follow up on than percent complete to see if the information was accurate. Second, it changed what had become a predictable communication pattern.

The previous example is not offered to turn you into a cynical or suspicious project manager. It is simply an example to show the power of changing your communication approaches. What project managers do not understand is that they allow themselves to get into a communication rut. This rut then conditions a team on how to communicate (and how to work the system, if they are inclined to do so). Regardless of their motivation, when communication methods become overly predictable and routine, people begin to communicate only in a certain way and only at certain times. It is important for project managers to mix up the types and ways they communicate with their project teams.

The issue log game, discussed in the next section, is another clear example of conditioned responses.

THE ISSUE LOG GAME

This is a game that both you and your team members may have played. Read the following scenario, from a team member's perspective:

It is a Tuesday afternoon and you are working on some paperwork when you hear a familiar sound coming from your computer, bringing your attention to a new window. The window is a calendar reminder that you have a status meeting in 15 minutes. A status meeting that you completely forgot about. You think you had something assigned to you, but can't remember. You quickly search through your e-mails and find the issue log that was published from the last meeting. You didn't open the issue log when it was sent because you thought to yourself, "I was just in that meeting; I don't need to read that!" You send out a quick e-mail and then go to the meeting.

The status meeting is the same as it always is. Everyone goes around the room reporting what percent complete they are and what they did or did not complete last week. Now it is time to discuss the issue log. The meeting finally gets to the issue that you were supposed to work on, but completely forgot about. The project manager asks you to provide the status. You look the project manager right in the eye and say, "I e-mailed Bob. I just haven't heard back yet." Of course you do not reveal that the e-mail to Bob is the quick e-mail that you sent right before the meeting. Technically, you are not lying!

This is the issue log game. It is a game that is perpetuated by the communication rut. During the research for my book *Project Management That Works!*, I discovered that roughly 80 percent of issues and problems were resolved in five business days. The reason? Status meetings are typically held every five business days. The issues or problems were identified in one status meeting and then resolved by the next meeting.

This is just one of many examples of why project managers need to change their communication methods and approaches. Mix them up. Do not just hold one status meeting and send out the same documentation every week. For those of you who have been conditioned over time to create a communication plan and follow it, please do not become alarmed! I am not suggesting that the practice is wrong. You must absolutely create a communication plan and follow it to the letter. As stated at the beginning of this chapter, it is essential to communicate often and control the message to avoid the grapevine effect. However, make sure that you are mixing up your communications so that you do not create a rut and allow the issue log game (or any other games, for that matter) to occur.

6 The Right Price

You can have the biggest circus on the street, but it comes down to price and having the right price.

– Martin Bouma

I think it's a great fit at the right price. At a high price it's a lousy deal, but at a lower price, it's a great deal.

– Andy Collins

The right price is a game played between a client and vendor in trying to negotiate a contract for work. The game essentially involves two simple questions:

Client: How much does this cost?

Vendor: How much do you have?

We all know why the game is being played. The client doesn't want to reveal how much money there is because of a fear the vendor will just create a quote that is one dollar less than the amount stated. The vendor doesn't want to reveal the potential cost because of a fear that whatever amount they say may price them out of the game. For instance, if the vendor pitches $100,000 and the client's budget is only $20,000, the client may stop the negotiations. This discussion usually happens early in the relationship—typically at the first meeting, before there has been a detailed examination of what the client needs. There could very well be a legitimate project that would suit the client's needs and that could be completed for $20,000, but because the vendor doesn't know what the client is asking for, they really do not know what to pitch. So this game of mistrust begins. The client is very reserved about the overall budget. The vendor is very reserved about how much everything will cost. In the meantime, valuable time is being wasted. This game is counterproductive for both parties.

The right price game is not reserved for external vendors. It is also played internally between departments. For example, project managers often have difficulty getting estimates from team members. The team members do not want to give specific estimates because they are afraid that they will actually be held to them. When I interviewed many team members about why they are reluctant to make estimates, most of the answers stemmed from mistrust between the project manager and the resource. Many team members stated that they did not have enough information to provide a proper estimate, or that they were afraid there would be negative consequences if they were wrong, or that they have been burned in the past by presenting estimates.

It is essential that team members and project managers come together to create valid estimates and write proper plans. So how do we stop the game? If mistrust seems to be the reason this game exists, then new tools must be created to establish trust faster. Obviously, in new relationships, trust is not easily given. Yet trust is needed to strike the appropriate balance so that everyone provides information quickly, and in a way that reflects the best interest of the project. The pricing estimator, discussed next, is a progressive approach to stop the games between clients and external vendors or between project managers and their resources.

PRICING ESTIMATOR

The Information Technology Infrastructure Library (ITIL) methodology utilizes a great concept called a service catalog. The service catalog establishes service-level agreements (SLAs) between an organization's business and IT departments so that the customers' expectations match the organization's delivery. What makes this service catalog so successful is that it forces the business and the IT departments to sit down and understand the constraints of both areas of the organization. The IT department has an opportunity to explain the activities it needs to perform in order to meet the business expectations. The business department has an opportunity to understand the length of time and amount of effort required to meet its needs. The goal is for the business and IT departments to reach common ground and ensure the organization achieves the right service level for the appropriate price.

The pricing estimator is a variation on this concept. It is a spreadsheet-based tool that allows two parties (clients and vendors, project managers and team members, or sponsors and the project team) to establish an understanding of what a project may involve in terms of scope, time, and cost. When being considered for a project, a vendor is often requested to create a fixed price contract based on very limited knowledge of the price involved. If the vendor is awarded the fixed price contract, oftentimes more work or more definition is revealed during the project, which causes the vendor to submit change requests or to try to increase the fixed price cost. This type of activity feeds the mistrust between the client and the vendor. It is the same mistrust that can be found between the project manager and the team member or the sponsor and the project team when time estimates are requested.

To combat these areas of mistrust, the vendor must provide the client with enough information so that the client can appropriately balance the deliverables requested for a satisfactory cost. Likewise, team members must provide enough information to their project manager so that the appropriate timeframes can be estimated. This is where the pricing estimator comes in. The pricing estimator is a blend of a service-level agreement template, PERT estimates, and scope definition. The goal of the pricing estimator is to allow the business or project manager to "back into" the appropriate number or timeframe with adjustments to the scope.

There are several steps involved in creating a pricing estimator. First, it is important to identify the activities needed to complete the work. For instance, if the vendor is implementing a standard off-the-shelf software package, the work may include:

- Plan the design
- Create a custom process
- Create a custom portlet
- Create a database trigger
- Create custom objects
- Create custom fields
- Create custom views
- Test
- Install
- Perform project setup and management
- Provide training

Once this list has been created, two things can occur. The first is to have the resources complete a three-point estimate for each item on the list. For example, a design meeting (part of the "plan the design item") can have a best-case time estimate of half an hour, most likely estimate of one hour, and a worst-case estimate of two hours. It is perfectly acceptable to have wide-ranging estimates between the best case and worst case, to show the variability of the estimate. A great example of this is the creation of a complex database trigger that could have a best-case estimate of one hour and a worst-case estimate of forty hours depending on the complexity of the work required. Once the three point estimates have been received, they can be loaded into a spreadsheet to help calculate an overall time or cost estimate.

The second thing is for the client or project manager to establish a more detailed list of activities required to complete the project. Defining the activities required establishes scope and provides both parties with the key information they need to know to stop the pricing game. In using the pricing estimator, the vendor or team member is being forthright by providing a range for the amount of time they need per activity to complete the work as they currently understand it. The client or project manager can then provide details for the scope of the activities. Both parties take turns exchanging information about scope, time, and cost in such a way that all of the typical unknowns become known.

To illustrate this technique further, let's look at a pricing estimator in action. In the following example, the client has asked for an initial quote from a consultant to install a project and portfolio management system. The consultant provides the following information:

General Tasks	Best Case (in hours)	Most Likely (in hours)	Worst Case (in hours)	PERT (in hours)
Project Setup and Management	2	4	8	4
Installation	4	8	16	9
System Architecture	8	16	24	16
Detailed Design	8	24	40	24
Security	40	60	80	60
Configuration Activities for Each Module	**Best Case (in hours)**	**Most Likely (in hours)**	**Worst Case (in hours)**	**PERT (in hours)**
Module Design Meetings	0.5	1	2	1
Process Development	1	3	8	4
Portlet Development	0.5	8	24	9
Trigger/Stored Proc. Development	1	8	40	12
Custom Objects	1	8	16	8
Custom Fields	0.25	0.5	1	1
Custom Views	0.25	0.5	1	1
Testing	1	2	3	2
Training Activities	**Best Case (in hours)**	**Most Likely (in hours)**	**Worst Case (in hours)**	**PERT (in hours)**
Executive Training	1	2	4	2
Project Manager Training	4	8	16	9
Resource Manager Training	2	4	8	4
Team Member Training	1	2	4	2
On-site Guidance	8	8	8	8

Table 1.1

The client then fills out all items in the light gray columns in the following tables. The client first determines which of the tasks to include in the project (table 2.1). Table 2.2 shows the six different modules involved in the project. The client enters data for each of the configuration activities associated with the modules. In table 2.3, the client indicates the amount of training they feel their employees will need.

Activities to Be Included in This Project (1 for Yes, 0 for No)	Yes or No
Project Setup and Management	1
Installation	1
System Architecture	1
Detailed Design	1
Security	0

Table 2.1

Module	Design Meeting	Process Dev.	Portlet Dev.	Trigger Dev.	C Objects	C Fields	C Views	Testing
Demand Management	1	2	0	0	1	10	1	2
Resource Management	1	0	1	2	0	12	1	3
Project Management	1	2	0	1	1	10	3	3
Portfolio Management	1	1	1	0	0	11	1	2
Financial Management	1	0	0	1	0	12	1	1
Requirements/ Release Management	1	0	0	0	0	5	1	0

Table 2.2

Training Activities	Sessions Needed
Executive Training	1
Project Manager Training	2
Resource Manager Training	4
Team Member Training	10
On-site Guidance Days (Full Days)	0

Table 2.3

The client and the consultant then agree on an hourly rate. With the rate determined, the information in the following tables can be shown:

Activities Included	Best Case		Most Likely		Worst Case		PERT Hours	Cost
	Hours	Cost	Hours	Cost	Hours	Cost		
Project Setup and Management	2	$480	4	$960	8	$1,920	4.3	$1,040
Installation	4	$960	8	$1,920	16	$3,840	8.7	$2,080
System Architecture	8	$1,920	16	$3,840	24	$5,760	16.0	$3,840
Detailed Design	8	$1,920	24	$5,760	40	$9,600	24.0	$5,760
Security	0	$0	0	$0	0	$0	0.0	$0
Total	22	$5,280	52	$12,480	88	$21,120	53.0	$12,720

Table 3.1

Module	Best Case		Most Likely		Worst Case		PERT Hours	Cost
	Hours	Cost	Hours	Cost	Hours	Cost		
Demand Management	8.3	$1,980	24.5	$5,880	51.0	$12,240	26.2	$6,290
Resource Management	9.3	$2,220	37.5	$9,000	128.0	$30,720	47.9	$11,490
Project Management	10.8	$2,580	35.5	$8,520	96.0	$23,040	41.5	$9,950
Portfolio Management	7.0	$1,680	22.0	$5,280	52.0	$12,480	24.5	$5,880
Financial Management	3.8	$900	7.5	$1,800	15.0	$3,600	8.1	$1,950
Requirements/ Release Management	2.0	$480	4.0	$960	8.0	$1,920	4.3	$1,040
Total	41.0	$9,840	131.0	$31,440	350.0	$84,000	152.5	$36,600

Table 3.2

Training Activities	Best Case		Most Likely		Worst Case		PERT Hours	Cost
	Hours	Cost	Hours	Cost	Hours	Cost		
Executive Training	1	$240	2	$480	4	$960	2.2	$520
Project Manager Training	8	$1,920	16	$3,840	32	$7,680	17.3	$4,160
Resource Manager Training	8	$1,920	16	$3,840	32	$7,680	17.3	$4,160
Team Member Training	10	$2,400	20	$4,800	40	$9,600	21.7	$5,200
On-site Guidance Days (Full Days)	0	$0	0	$0	0	$0	0.0	$0
Total	27	$6,480	54	$12,960	108	$25,920	58.5	$14,040
Total Estimate	90.0	$21,600	237.0	$56,880	546.0	$131,040	264.0	$63,360

Table 3.3

All parties benefit from the massive amount of information that is collected in this process. Without this tool, three or four or even five meetings are typically required for organizations to get to the level of detail shown in the previous tables. But the pricing estimator helps achieve this level of detail in the very first meeting and gives both parties a chance to begin to absorb the information shown. In the examples provided, you see a wide range of estimates. The total estimate range is between $21,600 and $131,040. The first thing the client is going to want to know is how to get toward the $21,600 range, and the consultant should want the client to ask how to ensure the best case. That question allows for a discussion with the client about risk management and the risks involved in implementation. If the consultant simply requested a risk meeting, most likely the client would not accept or attend. However, the pricing estimator shows the intrinsic value of a risk meeting to the client so they can begin to understand how they can affect the cost of their own project.

In addition, through the use of the pricing estimator and the accompanying discussions, the consultant is receiving clear and documented activity requirements. This is a refreshing change from what is many times the norm, in which the total amount of work is unknown. As the work begins in such cases, it becomes clear that what was estimated does not match what is required. These types of discrepancies can create very frustrating conversations and tension between the two parties. By using the estimator, however, the consultant has received defined requirements for each activity selected to be part of the project.

In the example shown, a total of four database triggers were identified in the initial meeting. But after the design meetings, fifth and sixth database triggers were identified. Had the parties not used the pricing estimator, an argument would have begun about the semantics of the request. Phrases such as, "That was what I meant," or "That was assumed," would have been used, and there would need to be concessions made by one of the two parties. But because the estimator was used, it was very clear that only four database triggers were initially identified. The clarity of the information enabled a smoother conversation about a necessary change in scope to add the two database triggers.

The level of information featured in the pricing estimator can be overwhelming, but it does reflect the complexity of the negotiations between the two parties. As they start discussing the data, the parties can make some immediate clarifications to achieve a common understanding. In this example, the client and consultant can immediately agree upon the exact length of time for the training sessions. Once that agreement has been established, the spreadsheet can be updated and the cost can be brought more in line with the expectations of both parties. Such agreements and discussions can continue until the contract terms and conditions are clarified.

One of the greatest benefits of utilizing the estimator is that it can be given to a client as an aid to select the number of activities that coincides with the number they had in mind for the budget for the overall project. The client does not have to reveal the number, and the consultant does not have to make a guess as to how much something is going to cost without enough information. As a result, the risk is removed for both parties.

Even though the example is showing a negotiation between a client and consultant, the same spreadsheet and the same information can be used internally between a project manager and a resource, or better yet, between a sponsor and the project team. For most departments in most organizations, even though a project is creating a unique service, product, or result, the activities being performed for different projects may not change dramatically. Therefore, for the common activities that each department or resource performs for projects, a standard estimate and activity can be defined in advance and placed in a spreadsheet like the one used for this example. This prepopulated spreadsheet then can be given to a sponsor or stakeholder to help them understand and balance their desires for both the content or scope of the project and the timeline for the project.

Think about the conversations that could come from this type of information. For instance, a sponsor could say, "I do not understand how to fill out the spreadsheet. I need more information or explanation as to what each activity means." The project manager can then use this conversation as an opportunity to help the sponsor understand the level of effort required to complete the requested project. If the sponsor becomes confused as to why an estimate could range from 1 hour to 1,000 hours for a single activity (and the confusion would be valid— this is too large of a variance), the project manager or resource has the chance to explain the variability they face in their day-to-day activities. All of these conversations can be utilized to help bring the sponsor's expectations and the project manager's or resource's expectations in line with each other.

HONEST CONVERSATIONS

As with many tools of project management, the pricing estimator is meant to serve as an aid and a guide to make the process easier. But it can't fix all problems and challenges. No matter the tool being used, honest conversations are still essential to success. For example, a consultant was called for an emergency consultation with a client. The client met with the consultant for one hour and requested pricing and the level of effort needed to complete a project. This is the same type of situation many people find themselves in when they are being asked to deliver a time estimate and do not have enough context to be able to estimate the effort appropriately. In this case, the consultant utilized the pricing estimator spreadsheet to document what he understood about the project and to present the potential range of estimates to the client.

At first, the client pushed back because they felt the spreadsheet was an overload of information and they simply wanted a price. The consultant explained that his intent in using the estimator was to give them a price and they could in fact use the PERT price supplied in the spreadsheet. However, if they had the opportunity to discuss the spreadsheet further, they could determine which items leaned more toward the best case and which items leaned more toward the worst case. As a result, a more refined price could be established.

The client agreed to schedule another meeting to discuss the estimate. In the 30-minute follow-up meeting that transpired, both parties agreed to a new scope of work and understanding of the project. The estimator helped them have honest conversations and served as the catalyst to discuss the needs of both parties.

A certain amount of trust is needed to achieve success. It takes courage for a team member or consultant to present best case, worst case, and most likely estimates. Therefore, every time a project manager communicates with someone on a project, he or she should remember to communicate from a standpoint of answering the team member's number one question: "What's in it for me?" Why should a resource give the project manager these types of estimates? Why should a consultant provide what would be considered intellectual capital in a spreadsheet?

An honest conversation can help build trust. From a resource's perspective, he or she must understand that giving estimates is the only way a project manager can help control the work/life balance, and if the resource fails to give explicit estimates, he or she must live with the implicit ones. For most companies, when it comes to projects, if there are no estimates provided, they will create their own estimates that suit them best. A project manager needs to convince team members that if they give proper estimates, the project manager can utilize the data to establish a more realistic and likely date. Without the information, the project manager has no data to present to the sponsor or stakeholders to truly show how long a project will take.

Likewise, in the client-vendor relationship, a vendor should be able to help alleviate the fear that they are there to charge as much as possible by providing this type of data to a client. Having the data in a spreadsheet format provides a proverbial line in the sand required to get both sides to discuss what they really need. If the honest conversations are held utilizing the data presented in the estimator, a base of trust is built and the contract negotiation can truly be win-win.

FIXED PRICE VERSUS TIME AND MATERIAL CONTRACTS

I created the pricing estimator process described in this chapter when I was forced to give a fixed price estimate to a client who provided little detail. There are many companies willing to provide fixed price estimates, however, when there is not nearly enough information to be able to do so with any confidence. Giving or using such estimates for either fixed price or time and material contracts has led to a perceived need to play games. Some companies do not like time and material contracts because they feel the vendor will not be as efficient, resulting in an increased total cost of the contract. Some vendors do not like fixed price contracts because they feel the client will try to get more work completed than agreed upon. Again, honest conversations and the use of the pricing estimator can alleviate these fears and build trust. Let's take a moment to look at both styles of contracts and the games that are played around them. Knowing such information can help you choose the best contract to fit your needs within your projects.

Most organizations prefer a fixed price contract because they feel it protects them from cost overruns. This feeling comes from having a known price for a known scope of work. However, there are many vendors out there who have mastered how to win a fixed price contract while creating enough ambiguity to allow multiple change requests to be added on later. For example, a company asks for a fixed price contract to implement a new widget. The vendor knows the cost will be $100,000 to implement the widget. However, the vendor also knows the lowest-cost provider will win the bid. Therefore, the vendor pitches $75,000 to win the contract and then creates change requests worth $25,000 during the project to get to the overall price of $100,000. Although we would like to believe this does not occur, it happens much more often than we realize.

On the other side of the negotiation, there are companies that know the work they want completed is worth $150,000, yet they will force a contract to a fixed price of $100,000. They will then use several negative tactics to try to get the vendor to throw in the other $50,000 needed, while still only paying the agreed-upon price of $100,000. Both examples are very unscrupulous; unfortunately they are also very common.

In a time and material contract, the fear is that the vendor will intentionally call additional meetings, delay the creation of documents, and create disarray in order to expand the timeframe and ultimately bill the company for more hours. Likewise, a company will hold a final invoice and not pay it due to a technicality. Since the product has already been delivered when they receive the final invoice, the company will drag on this negotiation in the hope of never having to pay the invoice. Again, these examples are very unscrupulous but very common.

The best way to initiate an honest conversation and avoid these types of games and unscrupulous activities is to utilize tools such as the pricing estimator. The estimator establishes a best case, most likely, and worst case timeframe and budget, which forces the different parties—vendor and client, project manager and team member, or sponsor and project team—to be truly honest with each other. The estimator also forces the client or sponsor to commit to the number of activities necessary to complete the project. Unscrupulous activities can still occur, but information has now been provided that can be used to control the project. For those who are walking the proper line, the estimator will help them establish trust and make the negotiations go faster.

7 Hit the Rodent

It can be very frustrating. Using scheduling tools are like playing Whac-a-Mole®. Every time I fix one thing, two others pop up!

– Dixie Fontenot

Hit the Rodent is a game many project managers play when trying to use scheduling tools. Whether they are utilizing Microsoft® Project, Open Workbench, or any of the other tools on the market to create a project schedule, they have a sense of sheer frustration over the use of these tools. So what is the Hit the Rodent game? Imagine this scenario. You have created a brand-new project plan, created activities, assigned the durations, and entered resources. When you add a second resource to an activity, all of a sudden the duration is cut in half— an automated feature of the software, popping up like a rodent head. You swing and hit the rodent by resetting the duration to the desired timeframe, but the work now doubles; a new rodent head pops up. You swing and hit this new rodent head and move the duration back to the desired amount. Now the dates move past your expected dates—yet another rodent head. By this point, you're extremely frustrated, so instead of utilizing the tool, you manually begin to enter the dates as if you are creating a spreadsheet. But the problem with manually entering dates is that it overrides the automated checks and other features of the tool that you actually wanted to take advantage of and now you are unable to trust the data provided.

This is a very common and frustrating game for many project managers. Most project managers are simply given a scheduling tool without training or without understanding how it really works. Scheduling tools are designed to take in a tremendous amount of data and show the impact, relationships, and true timeline of the entire project. When data is manually entered into certain columns in some of these tools, there are constraints, formulas, and other items automatically set within the tool that can cause even more frustration for the project manager. However, a scheduling tool is an absolute must for project managers. Scheduling tools are the only way to truly analyze, select, and report the progress of a project in today's fast-paced world. It is time to learn the rules of the game so you can eradicate the popping rodent heads forever.

LEARN THE TOOL!

It is an absolute guarantee—for every hour you spend learning and understanding the scheduling tool that you have, you will significantly reduce the amount of time and frustration involved in creating and managing your project plans. First, you need to understand the underlying formula for how work, duration, and dates are selected. The majority of project tools utilize this formula: Work = Duration × Units. The duration is entered for each activity and is expressed in days, weeks, or months. The units number indicates each resource's availability and is generally represented as a percentage of their day dedicated to the project. For example, if a resource is 100 percent dedicated to the project and has the availability of eight hours per day, then the number utilized for units is eight hours. Once the duration and units numbers are known, the work can be calculated. If an activity will take eight hours (duration), and the resource is assigned to 50 percent availability each day (units), then the work will equal two days.

Once this formula has been completed for the first time, the tool uses automated features to keep the formula in balance if any changes are made. For instance, if the project manager changes the two-day activity described earlier to four days, then either the work or the units percentage must be adjusted to keep the existing formula in balance. Many project managers are not only unaware of the formula, but they are also unaware that they must provide another piece of information to help balance the formula. So if the project manager increases the duration to four days but decides that the work is fixed (meaning that eight hours of work is all the activity will take, regardless of how many days the activity spans), the tool will reduce the units to 25 percent. This means the resource will spend 25 percent of his or her time each of the four days completing the activity, for a total of eight hours of work. These calculations can be confusing, but once you understand them, you have a very powerful knowledge base that allows you to rely on the data in your schedule with great confidence.

The project manager can generally control two types of options in a scheduling tool. The tool then automatically adjusts all of the other information to account for the selected designations. This means the project manager must choose whether an activity will have a fixed duration, fixed work, or fixed units, and whether or not the activity will be effort-driven. Let's explore these terms a bit further:

Fixed Duration
When the duration of an activity is fixed, it means that when the other items are adjusted, the tool will not adjust the duration number. The fixed duration option is most widely used in environments where resources work on multiple projects. If a resource requests two weeks to

complete an activity, the project manager would use fixed duration to appropriately show that within the schedule.

Fixed Units

When the units number is fixed, it means that the tool will not adjust the units of a resource if other information is changed. This option is utilized in environments where the resource has only a limited amount of time to work on the project each day.

Fixed Work

The fixed-work designation generally means that the work can be divided between multiple resources. If a project manager is looking for options to shorten the schedule and assigns additional resources to a fixed-work activity, the tool will generally shorten the duration of that activity.

Effort Driven

An effort-driven activity is synonymous with a fixed-work activity. Most project scheduling tools include this option so that the other items (duration or units) can also be fixed, telling the software to adjust the third item. This option can be very powerful when crashing a project schedule. To crash a project schedule, you add resources to an activity in order to shorten its duration. Painting a fence is an example of an effort-driven activity. If the fence takes eight hours to paint, adding a second resource will enable the eight hours of work to be performed in half the time. In contrast, a non-effort-driven activity means that the duration will not adjust even if more resources are placed on the activity.

For example, if the activity is to drive to Nashville, and the drive takes three hours, adding a second resource will not decrease the time it takes to get to Nashville.

To help illustrate this point further, let's look at this chart:

If the Activity Type Is:

		Fixed Units	Fixed Duration	Fixed Work
If You Change the Value of:	Units	The scheduling tool automatically adjusts: **Duration**	The scheduling tool automatically adjusts: **Work**	The scheduling tool automatically adjusts: **Duration**
	Duration	The scheduling tool automatically adjusts: **Work**	The scheduling tool automatically adjusts: **Work**	The scheduling tool automatically adjusts: **Units**
	Work	The scheduling tool automatically adjusts: **Duration**	The scheduling tool automatically adjusts: **Units**	The scheduling tool automatically adjusts: **Duration**

There are also other features in scheduling tools that can create frustration for people. For instance, have you ever tried to use predecessors and had the date on one activity refuse to automatically adjust when you entered in new information? The reason this happened is likely because the activity was manually entered in, thereby setting a constraint within the tool. For several of the scheduling tools on the market, if you enter a date in the Start column, it automatically sets a constraint of "Start No Earlier Than" the date you entered. The same happens for the Finish column. If a date is entered in that column, a constraint will be assigned as "Finish No Earlier Than." When the project manager comes back to work on the plan, and the dates do not seem to adjust the way he or she anticipated, the sense of frustration erupts.

There are some general rules to creating schedules in these tools that must be followed to ensure you are getting the most value from the tools:

- Do not manually enter any dates. (There is even a place in most tools to set the start date so that it is not manually entered in the activity information.)

- Every activity except for the very first activity should have a predecessor. This will ensure that the schedule will "ebb and flow" as activities finish early or late.

- Define the durations. Some tools allow you to enter dates, and then the tools try to assume the actual duration. Make sure the duration is exposed and you are the one setting it.

- Baseline, baseline, baseline. You must baseline the schedule to get the full value of the tool.

If you spend time learning to use your scheduling tool, you will recoup that time whenever you update the project plan and you will be able to confidently rely on the data that is provided by the tool.

DATA = GETTING WHAT YOU NEED

If you do not have the data, how do you know what you need? If you do not have a schedule set up appropriately, how can you possibly know when the project is going to be completed? If you have been manually entering dates into a scheduling tool, or using a spreadsheet, and the activities are not linked together the way they should be, then you cannot be confident in the data you have and you are not truly aware of the project schedule. It is simply impossible to try to manage all of the contingencies, possibilities, and deviations with any sense of accuracy if the project scheduling tool is not used properly.

In contrast, if you have set up the scheduling tool appropriately, you can utilize the data to influence the context of the project. In an earlier chapter, we discussed the value of using assumptive statements. These statements are posed as either/or questions instead of yes/no questions. In order to get the data necessary to make such assumptive statements, having a real (and reliable) project schedule is paramount. Being able to quickly and effectively show a sponsor the impact of his or her decisions will increase your credibility as a project manager and also increase the value and power of the assumptive statements.

Many project managers get excited upon hearing there is a way to fix or influence some of the situations that are forced upon them in organizations. But the principles being utilized to fix the situations are the same principles that many of us have been taught from day one. The principles of project management, the reasons these principles were established, and how they work, can and do impact the project management landscape. The number one reason for project failure is abandoning these principles.

In order to put all of the information into a scheduling tool to accurately calculate the data used in making assumptive statements, you should have the following:

- A project scope statement

- A full work breakdown structure (WBS)

- Estimates from all resources

- A network diagram showing the dependencies between activities

- An understanding of the level of effort or the commitment level for each resource

Did you notice that a WBS was included in the previous list? For many project managers, a work breakdown structure is simply an answer on an exam. Project managers often report that they have never done a WBS in the real world, or they state that their company will not allow such an activity to occur. Many project managers simply do not know how to get one started, or they have never had a chance to practice using this tool and do not want their first attempt at creating a WBS to be at their company. Work breakdown structures do work, and they are a necessary tool to understanding what's involved in your project. If you want to practice creating a WBS outside of your place of employment, here is a great tip: Seek out a charity, such as a church or other nonprofit organization, and volunteer your time. Tell them you are a practicing project manager and would like to utilize a technique that you have been trained in to help them organize their next activity or project. They will relish this opportunity, and it will provide a fantastic learning experience for you. (One word of warning: volunteering in such a way can be quite infectious; you may find yourself wanting to do it again!)

So make sure you are using the tools of project management, including a WBS, to gather the data necessary to create an accurate and reliable schedule. If the rodent heads seem to keep popping up no matter what you do when creating the schedule and you cannot figure out how to prevent this, you must invest in learning how to use your scheduling software. There are phenomenal resources available, many of which focus on scheduling tools in particular, including books, Web-based learning, training classes, and coworker knowledge. Understanding how to create a proper project schedule can increase your project success rate exponentially.

DON'T FORCE IT!

As a common rule of thumb in any game, you do not want to force something to happen. If a square peg will not fit into a round hole, forcing it will only damage the peg and the hole. Likewise, trying to force the scheduling tool to hit the date that you have in your head can have the same effect. And forcing management to look at the tool further, arguing with them about the dates, or refusing to accept what they have said can turn you into the rodent that they want to hit. There is a three-step process to making sure you get your point across without turning yourself into a rodent head.

Step One: Establish Your Mindset

This first step—establishing your mindset—means you need to be prepared to have the conversation not go your way. For most people, if the conversation is going in a different direction than they had hoped, their internal resistance flares up and begins to make a negative impact. In contrast, you must establish a mindset that you are not going to be combative, argumentative, or disrespectful in the negotiations. You are simply going into the meeting to present facts, push the decision to the executives, and execute the decision that is made.

Step Two: Get to the Data

By following the techniques in this chapter, you should have collected the data you need to present. Make sure you have gone through the data several times and that you trust the information you are about to present. Data absolutely rules all. If you have more of it, and it is completely accurate, you will win in the long run.

Step Three: Accept the Answer

This can be the hardest step of all. You want to see a resolution that goes in your favor. However, it doesn't always happen as you hope. Even if the decision that has been provided to you is the most ridiculous decision that has ever been made, you must be prepared to accept it. Document the request, the data presented, and the outcome of the meeting. Every time you request a decision from the sponsors or executive team, you must document the outcome. Documenting the decision is creating a new data stream you can rely upon later to help influence the outcome you desire at the next negotiation. Analyzing these decisions in retrospect will begin to change the organizational culture over time.

This three-step process can truly give you peace of mind in project management while helping to establish a healthy culture in your organization.

Some who read this will ask how accepting the answer that is given will change culture. One way that it can immediately affect the culture is when the organization has to answer the question, "Why did this project fail?" With the three-step system, you have the documentation of how it failed. You have recorded the baselined schedule, the data you presented to management, the decisions that were made, and the outcome of the project. This data will create a new stream of analysis that can lead to long-term, permanent change. You will be able to refer to the collected data as further proof of what was needed. Conversations like the following can occur:

PM: "We need to add three more resources, or the date will slide to July 30."

Executive: "We do not have three resources to give to the project."

PM: "So then we're looking at the date of July 30."

Executive: "No, the date has to be June 15."

PM: "The last three times we have been in this position, we have missed the date and had a conversation as to why the date was missed. We really need to look at what the data is telling us."

Executive: "We have failed the last three times?"

PM: "We have missed the date that you and I set the last three times."

Executive: "Let's have another look at that plan."

Using the reliable data available from a properly set-up scheduling tool and then documenting the negotiation and the results of the negotiation make a powerful argument for change.

8 | Marco! Polo!

If you don't know where you are going, any road will get you there!

– Lewis Carroll

A good plan, violently executed now, is better than a perfect plan next week.

– General George S. Patton

Ever feel completely lost on a project? Do you sometimes not know if you are coming or going? It's like you are screaming, "Marco!" and praying that you hear, "Polo!" And then the problem is that you do hear it coming, but from 17 different directions. One of the most commonly used phrases as an argument against project management is, "We do not have time to plan; we have to get going."

Think of what it was like for explorers, sailing off to unchartered lands. Even when the explorers did not know what the voyage would hold for them, they knew the direction they were heading. Of course, they were also recording the data of how to get home. Now imagine you are trying to sail the vast expanse of the ocean without a compass or the sun to guide you. Every day you wake up, work, and sail until the sun goes down. You put in the right amount of effort each day. However, you are completely unaware if the day brought you closer to or further away from your target, or if you sailed one direction one day and in the complete opposite direction the next day. Without a map, without a plan, the voyage is pointless.

Many project managers suffer a similar fate. They are forced to go forward without a plan. And to make matters worse, they often do not fully understand the reason why their project was undertaken in the first place. Even in these situations, project managers must document where they have been so they know how to work with the next set of circumstances they will face.

A PLAN IS A MUST

A plan is an absolute must. There is no project management without clear direction and a plan. Even if we are instructed to work without a plan or do not have the ability to create the plan in the beginning, a plan must be created. Of course we all want to perform the process. We want to utilize the principles of project management and create a schedule that is realistic and achievable. This is done through the following actions:

- Create a scope statement
- Create a work breakdown structure
- Define activities and then sequence them
- Get time and cost estimates
- Develop a schedule
- Perform qualitative and quantitative risk analysis to establish contingencies
- Add contingencies back into the schedule and publish it

Many organizations that lack maturity in project management try to jump from creating the scope statement to developing and publishing the schedule. And some organizations do not even go that far. Here is the stark message for them: if there is not a WBS, and there are no reliable estimates, you cannot produce an accurate schedule. It is absolutely impossible to know when a project will be finished without these assets. If an organization is not going to follow the process, they may as well pick an end date by getting a large wall calendar that has the next three years on it and throwing a dart at it. They can then take whatever date it lands on and publish that. This may actually be more accurate than some of the other arbitrary methods used to pick dates. In chapter 4, we discussed the value of the phrase, "I don't know." If you find yourself in a conversation about an end date when there has been no planning effort, this is a good time to use it.

Let's look at a conversation where this was the case:

PM: "We will get started on planning this project."

Executive: "We do not have time to plan; we have to get started now. This project has to be done by June 15."

PM: "I need to create a WBS and get time estimates to let you know if June 15 is possible."

Executive: "June 15 is possible. You do not have a choice."

PM: "Without a plan and estimates, how do we know what it will take to hit June 15?"

Executive: "I have already committed to June 15. We do not have time for all of that project management mumbo jumbo. Do whatever it takes to get the job done."

PM: "I have no idea what it will take. Without a plan or estimates, we are just guessing. What did you use to come up with the date of June 15?"

Executive: "That is the date that I settled on."

PM: "So how did you figure out how long it would take?"

Executive: "I strive to push my people to their maximum potential. I find that if I push them, they will make it. You just have to have guts."

PM: "So you have no idea if June 15 is actually possible, and you won't let me spend the time it takes to find out if it is possible? I guess we can all just hope for the best."

Obviously, this is a pretty extreme conversation. It is also a real conversation. The unfortunate end to this story is that the project manager did not hit June 15, the company said they did not see the value of project management, and the project manager was let go.

There are many people who can share similar stories and similar results. So what can you do? The project manager in the previous example was boxed into a no-win situation. The organizational culture placed no value on project management and there was no room for the project manager to plan a project or put into practice project management principles. In such a situation, if you are going to go down anyway, go down swinging! If an executive is pushing you to run a project without a plan, you must use every opportunity to establish the context that proceeding would be like sailing on the vast expanse of an ocean with no compass and no idea if you will ever be successful. It will undeniably be an uphill battle, but so is simply complying with the demands. As noted earlier, this book is not suggesting that you become argumentative or combative. Instead, take every opportunity to use data to establish context in each situation and to document results in order to set up future conversations.

ACTING AS IF A MISTAKE IS NOT MADE

One of the most interesting stories in history is the discovery of America by Christopher Columbus. It has been taught that when he landed on the continent of North America, he thought he had hit India. He named the native people of the land "Indians." However, the people Columbus referred to as Indians called themselves Cherokee, Dakota, Navajo, etc. Although as a culture, we now often use the term "Native Americans," the term "Indians" is also commonly used. We continue to perpetuate the mistake.

Many projects operate the same way when it comes to perpetuating mistakes. The question of why projects fail is a highly sought-after topic of discussion. When I've given lectures on this topic, I've often asked, "How many people have been put on a project that they knew would fail the moment they received it?" You might be surprised by how many people raise their hands. The next question is, "How many of you were still forced to do the project?" A few hands drop, but not enough to change the statistical comparison. The final question is,

"How many of those projects actually failed?" Again, a few hands drop, but roughly 90 percent of the people who originally raised their hands still have them raised. This is ludicrous! Just like continuing to use a term that was never correct in the first place, we undertake projects that we understand are bound to fail—projects that are mistakes—yet we continue down the project path anyway. Why is that? How much time, money, and resources have we wasted in trying to complete something we knew would fail? The end result is staggering. So many organizations never seem to learn from the past mistakes and keep perpetuating the same mistakes over and over again. It could be an issue of corporate culture, or it could be a fear of challenging the company's leadership. In any case, it creates a waste cycle that is detrimental to an organization.

LOSING THE FOREST BECAUSE OF THE TREES

Many organizations lose the forest because of the trees. They do not see that the same mistake is being repeated. And the project managers within these organizations feel they are unable to change the behaviors leading to the mistake. But you can change corporate culture, and you can make a difference. It is up to you to paint the picture of the forest, even if you have to do it one tree at a time.

Project managers commonly report feeling powerless in their work. In some organizational cultures, project managers have been demoralized to the point that apathy begins to reign. It is time for a change. It is time to chart a new path and rise to the challenge of making a positive difference in your organization. Start by following the processes within this book. Make sure you have reliable data. In every situation, establish your mindset, present the data, and document the outcome. Remember that although you are responsible for the project, your job is not to make every decision on the project and ensure project success at any cost to your team and your sanity. Instead, your job is to manage the project, present options, and facilitate the resulting decisions.

One of the strangest project management misconceptions out there is the belief that project managers can guarantee a date. It is a belief that project managers can control time and space and make things happen. In corporate environments, how often do you suppose employees have actually dropped dead because a "drop dead" date passed? If people could look into the future and guarantee that dates would be met, they likely wouldn't be project managers. They would make more money and get more recognition as a psychic or stockbroker. It is impossible for us to see into the future. Project managers cannot guarantee dates. But given the opportunity to plan, they can determine the statistical probability of hitting a date, and they can determine what they feel needs to be done to hit a date.

So take solace in this fact. And for every date that is mandated, take down the following information:

- The date the project was given to you
- The mandated or requested finish date
- The date your analysis indicated the project would really be done (even if it is months later)
- The date the project was completed

As promoted repeatedly in this book, recording such information begins to build a data stream that can be utilized in negotiations and conversations with your sponsors. Having this information available at your fingertips is paramount in establishing the context of project management. You can then use the metrics to make statements such as:

- "We are 75 percent more likely to hit an agreed-upon date if you give me a couple more weeks to plan before committing to a date."
- "Historically, when we rush the planning activities, roughly four months elapse before we are sure of when the project will complete. By the time we know the completion date, 80 percent of the effort of the project has been expended. We would like to see if we could decrease that to 10 percent of the effort expended."

These are simple metrics, but powerful ones. If you have tracked and documented data properly, then you can begin to help chart the course for your organization. Even an organization that does not believe in project management will start to see the pattern and begin to recognize the value of properly planning a project. Each step into this new world should help reduce the uncertain cries of "Marco!" and the fragmented responses of "Polo!" on the organization's projects. Instead, project managers, their team members, and the organization as a whole will clearly understand the direction they are heading.

9 Armchair Quarterback

This is the old armchair quarterback theory. Everybody thinks they can be a better coach, a better general manager, a better owner.

– Greg Ambrosius

We think that [$3.8 billion] is actually a pretty conservative estimate, because it just takes into account time visiting Web sites, but you can't account for time people spend armchair quarterbacking.

– Rick Cobb, discussing the cost of the lost productivity of surfing the Internet at work

Armchair quarterbacking in project management means one project manager calling out another project manager. There is always a better way to do things. There is always an easier way to perform certain tasks. However, one project manager openly criticizing another project manager is just reckless. The criticism is often born from ignorance. The person performing the analysis is assuming he or she knows how everything went down.

But to truly understand the situation, the critic would have needed to be part of each meeting and know why each decision was made.

Let's look at an example of project management armchair quarterbacking. A project manager had been implementing a new project and portfolio management tool. The client was very rushed and wanted to see immediate results. The team had done a thorough analysis of the requirements and had provided a detailed project plan. The plan stated that the tool would be ready for use by the end of the second quarter. The executives stated that they liked the content of the project, but wanted to know what it would take to ensure a delivery of April 15. The team explained it was unlikely they could deliver the project in that timeline, but the executives pushed for a plan to meet the April 15 requirement. The team provided a charter and a plan with the following assumptions and constraints:

- The requirements would be "time-boxed," and design would only happen at the beginning of the project.
- Another team was working on a business process reengineering effort. The output of their process would be the input to the requirements of the project.
- The core team would be responsible for all key decisions.

- Scope would be tightly managed. Any new requirements not already identified would be included in the next phase of the project.

- All resources on the team would be 100 percent dedicated to this effort.

- Due to the accelerated timeframe, only 80 percent of the requirements would be delivered.

The executives agreed, and the project was set in motion. When the project was completed, it was considered a failure. The actual results were as follows:

Assumption	Actual Occurrence
The requirements would be "time-boxed," and design would only happen in the beginning of the project.	Many items were designed and redesigned. The team made key decisions without input from the user, as stated within the charter, but every time the system was shown to the user, new requirements and designs were accommodated. The budget spreadsheet went through 24 revisions, yet it still did not seem to be right.

Assumption	Actual Occurrence
Another team was working on a business process reengineering effort. The output of their process would be the input to the requirements of the project.	The business process reengineering effort was not completed. The team never received the inputs.
The core team would be responsible for all key decisions.	Many decisions were made outside of the core team.
Scope would be tightly managed. Any new requirements not already identified would be included in the next phase of the project.	Scope was not tightly managed. When the team would push back on new requirements or significant changes, they were put under a lot of top-down pressure to make the changes.
All resources on the team would be 100 percent dedicated to this effort.	Only 2 of the 24 people assigned to the project remained on the project full-time. The other 22 were either removed, the time they could work on the project was reduced, or they were switched for other resources throughout the project.

Assumption	Actual Occurrence
Due to the accelerated timeframe, only 80 percent of the requirements would be delivered.	The team delivered 132 percent of the requirements.

The context of what happened throughout the project is hard to fully understand without having been a part of the team. One of the key occurrences was that the project's sponsor was removed at the end of the project and a new person was placed in that role. The new sponsor was one of the people whom the project charter excluded from the decisions. This is where the armchair quarterbacking began.

On paper, the project was actually a success. It was completed on time, over-delivered, and met the agreed-upon scope, even though every single documented assumption identified had been ignored or overridden. The end result was the consultant and the project manager on the project were removed, the core team people were let go, and other key stakeholders were reorganized. Instead of understanding the final challenges involved in implementing the software, the new sponsor decided to dump the project and start completely over with a new team. Unfortunately, this story is more the norm than the exception.

YOU MIGHT REAP WHAT YOU SOW

Prior to the consultant and primary project manager's removal, there were several questions posed by a new project manager assigned to the project. This is where the armchair quarterbacking can get ugly for all project managers. First, let's look at the questions posed, the initial responses, and the armchair quarterback statement:

Question	Initial Response	Armchair Quarterback Statement
Was the user community involved in making the decision?	No.	All projects need to include the users of the system to flush out proper requirements.
Was there a testing plan?	Yes.	
Was the testing plan followed?	No.	I never put in a project without completing a full testing plan.
Was there a change control process established?	Yes.	
Was the change control process followed?	No.	I can see why you guys failed.

Several more of these types of questions were posed. The consultant answered each one of them openly and honestly. At each answer, the new project manager provided commentary trying to establish her superiority over the consultant and the outgoing project manager. At the end of the interrogation, the consultant questioned the new project manager, and she got to reap what she had sown.

> **Consultant:** "When you are told to do something by your boss, as long as it is not breaking moral codes or asking you to break the law, do you do it?"

> **New PM:** "Yes."

> **Consultant:** "So if your boss and your project charter told you to not interview the project community, would you do what your project charter, which establishes your authority, and your boss said, or do you interview them anyway because you "always" get them?"

> **New PM:** "I guess I do what my boss says."

> **Consultant:** "Our charter told us to not interview the users. Now, you say that you never submit a project plan without a full testing plan. Can you show me one of yours?"

> **New PM:** "Uh, um, uh, I don't have one that I can show you right now."

Consultant: "You said earlier that you keep all of your files on your laptop in case you ever need them, so if you do not have a test plan on your laptop, does this mean you do not actually have a test plan document that you used?"

New PM: "Um...I don't have one."

Consultant: "We established that all changes would go into a new phase of the project. When new requirements were made, we asked for them to wait. When management said no, we filled out a change control request. Management told us they would not accept the change control and to put the new requirement in the project immediately. We documented that we did all of those steps, but ultimately bent to the wishes of our management. What would you have done differently?"

New PM: "Um...I guess nothing."

The new project manager, once full of bravado, was no longer so confident. Nobody won this exchange. Ultimately, the consultant and outgoing project manager were replaced. They felt they did everything they could, but in the end, they did not meet the expectations of the organization. The new project manager was demoralized. She fell into the mistake that many of us face. Instead of finding out what had transpired on the project, she assumed that the consultant and project manager didn't know what they were doing. Instead of assuming they would have followed the process if they could have, she assumed they were ignorant of the process.

Here is another armchair quarterback example in which a consultant project manager calls out another consultant project manager. A project manager, whom we will call Steve, and his company had worked for over a year to secure a project. In the meantime, a salesperson from Steve's company left to work for a competitor. When Steve's company finally secured the project, the competitor had somehow inserted themselves into the role of project manager of the initiative. In essence, the competitor's project manager, whom we will call Sally, was now going to manage Steve's company's effort to deliver the initiative. This was a sure recipe for disaster. Steve contacted the sponsor and asked if utilizing Sally in this capacity was a conflict of interest. The sponsor was livid at the suggestion. Steve decided to accept the project against his better judgment. He typed a letter to the sponsor, signed it, had the letter date-stamped, and sent it with the instructions to open it at the end of the involvement of his organization.

The project began. The first milestone was due in March. In the December prior to the due date, Sally started calling delivery meetings to check progress. Although the first major milestone was not due for a few months, Steve agreed to show her the progress. After the first meeting, Sally called Steve to let him know how disappointing the first view was. Steve explained that they were ahead of schedule and were on track to deliver in March. Sally stated that March was no longer a good date and said the team had two weeks to deliver something more substantive. Steve and his team began to work around the clock. Every delivery and every step was met with disappointment and increasingly harsh criticism by Sally.

Steve finally had enough and called a meeting with the sponsor. The sponsor invited Sally. Steve stated that in order to be successful, he would need space on-site at the client's location, direct access to the client's resources, and access to the sponsor. All three requests were denied. However, Sally's organization was represented in a cubicle right outside of the sponsor's office and had direct access to the resources.

Steve and his team continued to work diligently. They delivered the first prototype four full months prior to the agreed-upon date. At that time, the sponsor informed Steve that Sally's organization would be performing the acceptance testing. Bug after bug was reported. When Steve's team closed a bug, Sally's team would reopen two more based off of the first one. The project became a never-ending game of armchair quarterback. At every step, Sally announced to the client why her organization was better. Eventually, Steve's company was replaced by Sally's company. This ended the involvement of Steve's organization. Steve was quite disappointed and felt powerless in trying to resolve the situation. The only thing Steve could do was to ask the sponsor to read the time-stamped letter. The letter read as follows:

To: Sponsor

Re: Conflict of Interest

At the beginning of this project, we raised the issue of a conflict of interest. Although you stated that there was no conflict present, I disagree. If you are reading this letter, then our involvement with the project has completed. My prediction is that we have been removed from the project due to a failure of some sort that has been raised by Sally. I also predict that the project has been awarded to Sally and her organization. If this is the case, I wish you the best of luck. If I am wrong and we have been allowed to successfully deliver this project, we will refund 10 percent of the overall price immediately as an apology for calling your integrity into question.

Sincerely,
Steve

This was a risky move. However, Steve had nailed it right on the head. The sponsor immediately began to question Sally's motives. Sally was then subjected to some of the same treatment she had inflicted on Steve's organization. She was asked to accelerate the project, could not have direct access to the resources she needed, and ultimately was removed from the project. Sally got to reap what she had sown.

Nobody won in this story. Steve, Sally, and the sponsor all lost credibility. Regardless of the circumstances, Steve did not deliver the project. Sally had her lack of integrity exposed and lost the project and a customer. The sponsor, after two failures, was ultimately let go. And all of this occurred for what reason? Can we simply blame Sally? The sponsor should have known better than to have a vendor manage a vendor. Steve should have followed his principles and not accepted the project after the conflict of interest was revealed. Sally destroyed her reputation by destroying another vendor and then not being able to deliver the project herself.

Nobody wins the armchair quarterback game. Regardless of the motivations of those playing it, it does not promote positive change in an organization. So be careful when analyzing lessons learned or taking over a failing project. Know that you cannot understand the full picture and make sure you do not affix blame or try to assume the current status. You may have to reap what you sow!

THERE IS NO CRYING IN PROJECT MANAGEMENT!

In order to successfully implement the practices promoted in this book, you need to have a passion and belief that things can change. Attitude is important. In the same way that armchair quarterbacking promotes a culture of blame and a general sense of negativity across an organization, a positive attitude is essential for positive change. You need to believe that organizations will learn from their mistakes and will make long-lasting changes. There are many who hear new theories and approaches and then state, "That will never work in my company." They may also say, "You obviously have never worked for a boss like mine." This book is not for those who believe change is impossible. It is directed at those who are willing to try new techniques and have the passion to use them correctly. Essentially, you have three choices. When an organization is failing to recognize the value of project management or the value of the process, you can:

1. Persevere

Try the new techniques. Have small wins, and continue to educate and motivate the organization. If people in the organization are unwilling to try new concepts, then you must work with them to answer questions such as, "What's in it for me?" or "Why should I want to change?" Change is not easy or quick. It takes true dedication and passion to effect long-term change. Persevering project managers continue to follow the process the best they can, educate others as often as possible, and improve the organization's effectiveness at every opportunity.

2. Accept

If you choose to accept, you are giving into the belief that the organization will not change. In this case, stop whining about it! If you are resolute that the organization will not change and that you will not make any movements to try to change it, then just accept the organization for what it is.

3. Move On

If you are resolute that the organization will not change and you feel that you can't operate within the organization, then move on. Go find an organization that you feel will suit you best.

There truly are only three choices. Once you understand this, you understand that there is no crying in project management! Recognizing these options and making a decision of which to pursue should remove any angst or ill will toward your organization as well. There is no reason to continue to complain or whine about the current organizational politics. If you do not like it, change it. If you can't change it, accept it. If you can't accept it, find a new organization.

ASSUME THE BEST

It is time that we take on a new view of other project managers. Instead of nitpicking them and questioning their every move, it is time that we build camaraderie within the profession. We all face similar challenges and similar circumstances. Why don't we assume the best of each other? One of the most commonly overlooked options is the option to choose. In every situation and interaction, knowingly or unknowingly, we choose to feel how we feel. This is a very powerful concept once you understand how to harness the power. Let's look at an example.

Someone just yelled to you, "Hey...idiot!" You turn around to see who shouted at you...and then you choose how you will react.

Situation 1: It is a long-time friend, and the insult is a joke and term of endearment. You just laugh and shout back, "Who are you calling idiot?" It is all in fun.

Situation 2: You don't know the person who shouted. You react by shouting back, "Who are you calling idiot?" It is not in fun or a jest—it is an escalating confrontation.

The point is that we affix connotation to almost every situation in life. Many times, we unknowingly choose a negative connotation and allow ourselves to become upset. Why is that?

Here is another example. You are a motivational speaker giving a speech. From the front of the room, you notice:

- A member of the audience is nodding off
- Someone just left the room
- Two people are whispering

You have two choices. The first choice is to assume each of these occurrences has something to do with you:

- A member of the audience is nodding off: "Man, I am boring him to death!"
- Someone just left the room: "I have offended her. She doesn't like me."
- Two people are whispering: "They have lost interest in my message."

Or, you can react the following way:

- A member of the audience is nodding off: "He had a really late night, but he is trying to make it through my presentation because he really wants to be here."
- Someone just left the room: "There is an emergency she needs to deal with."
- Two people are whispering: "They are sharing with each other how they will use the concepts tomorrow."

The truth is that you don't really know any of the reasons for the audience members' behavior. However, you can choose what connotation you want to place on the event. Since you are ultimately in control of the connotation, it doesn't have to be negative!

This idea is applicable to personal relationships as well. We often argue or disagree because of how we choose to take something versus what the intent was. For instance, imagine you have a family member that seems to always want to one-up the situation. He says things in an effort to try to get a reaction out of your spouse. If he can't get to her, then he tries to get to you. If he can't get to you, then he tries to get a reaction out of the other members of your family, and so on. It sometimes feels as if his joy in life is putting down you or your family. But what if you choose to affix a different connotation to the behavior? Who knows the reason for the behavior? You really don't. So instead of attaching negative feelings to it, you just shake your head and say, "That's odd" when you observe the behavior. You can then move on without losing energy or happiness over it.

In business, there are many fantastic motivators and project managers who would not be good direct managers. Their entire careers have been spent influencing people who did not report to them on an organization chart. When a project manager does have people report to him or her, the project manager may be awful at some of the key skill sets involved in directly managing others. For example, a project manager had a person report to him who seemed to believe he was out to get her. She placed a negative connotation on every action he performed. Some of her reactions were warranted and some were just plain unfair. He tried everything he could think of to build the relationship, but he was never successful. It bothered him for a very long time. Finally, he decided to choose what connotation he would affix to the situation. He looked at his efforts to rebuild the relationship and came to the realization that he had done enough. He could look at himself in the mirror and honestly state that he tried everything he could to make the relationship work. He let go of the negativity and hurt feelings and could happily move on.

Choosing how you take something is a very powerful technique. People will see somebody really happy and ask, "Why are they are so happy?" The answer is that they choose to be. You can make a decision to find the good in situations. It is time for you, as a project manager, to stop armchair quarterbacking. Stop assuming you have the full picture and instead start affixing positive connotations to other project managers and project management situations. When you take over a project, assume the previous project manager truly wanted to follow the process and principles of project management but for some reason was unable to. Instead of affixing a negative connotation to the person or the profession, you will then be able to direct your efforts at identifying what did not allow them to follow through so you can avoid the same issues. Leave the armchair quarterbacking to the sports fans who think they know it all.

Rules of the Game

You can't break the rules until you know how to play the game.

   – Rickie Lee Jones, American singer and songwriter

The trouble with referees is that they know the rules, but they do not know the game.

   – Bill Shankly, Scottish soccer player and manager

To play any game, you must know the rules. If you do not understand the rules, then you will likely look like you don't know what you are doing. This is true in business, too. There are many rules, many political events, many subtle communications that a person must understand and master in order to be successful. There are no shortcuts. There are no quick fixes to long-term project management or cultural change. So let's take a look at the undeniable rules that are so essential for change.

ALWAYS GET THE DATA

The first rule is to always get the data. Data rules all. It is the most important element in every negotiation, task, and strategic initiative. The one who has the most data, the best understanding of that data, and the most influential way to present it will come out ahead. If data is gathered and used appropriately, the decisions organizations need to make regarding key crossroad events and the factors that impact those decisions should become crystal clear. If faced with an unsure situation or a quality issue, find a way to measure it. Analyze the data, suggest a fix, and then measure it again once the fix is implemented. The new measurements will tell you if the fix was successful. Project managers have access to a compendium of tools and knowledge that should assist them in collecting the data they need. Work breakdown structures, network diagrams, schedules, issue and risk logs, variance or status reports, and many other such tools can help a project manager gather the appropriate information.

Let's look at an example of how people measured and used data to make a tremendous difference in their organization:

A health care company had recently put in a project management office (PMO). When the PMO first started, there were 183 projects on the active list and 5 project managers. The PMO followed the capacity model that was discussed in chapter 2 and determined that they had an incredible overallocation problem. Armed with this information, they approached the chief information officer (CIO) with the hopes that the company would hire new project managers. The CIO, who saw project management as a necessary evil instead of a practice that can become a strategic resource, said he would tap 30 functional managers to become "project leads." These project leads would then run projects. This was not the result the PMO had hoped for. But they followed the three-step process discussed in chapter 7; they collected data, presented it, and then accepted the repeated answer that there were going to be 30 project leads. They then determined what new data to track to show if the process would be successful.

The largest fear the PMO had regarding the 30 project leads was that it would take even more of the precious little time the 5 project managers had to mentor them. Therefore, when the team met to define a new way to capture data, they decided they would track time in categories and see if there was a correlation between the project success or failure and the time they spent in each one of the categories. The categories were as follows:

- **Planning:** How much time did the project manager spend actually planning each project that was worked on?

- **Administration:** How much time did the project manager spend filling out status reports, using project management systems, etc.?

- **Communication:** How much time did the project manager spend communicating? This includes meetings, hallway conversations, etc.

- **Mentoring:** How much time did the project manager spend mentoring the project lead on a project?

The end result of tracking this data was the PMO was able to show that very little time was spent actually planning, even with the involvement of the project leads. In fact, the data showed that the addition of the 30 project leads created more of a drain on resources and simply allowed the organization to do more projects poorly. However, in analyzing this data, a new and unexpected pattern emerged that led the PMO to come up with a way the organization could utilize the project lead concept and still be successful. The PMO proposed that the organization let the five project managers focus on the initial planning of the projects. The project managers would form the WBS, network diagram, and project schedule for each project. The project leads would then fill out the status reports, do the project administration, and attend many of the meetings. If a project began to slide, one of the project managers would intervene and help bring the project back on track. This proposal achieved the best balance of the project managers' time. It was approved by management. In tracking the data to see if the new approach was effective, the PMO found that a higher percentage of time was now spent on planning and the organization saw an immediate impact on project success statistics.

This example is one of many that show the value of taking a calm and calculated approach to change. Even when immediate decisions do not go your way, take a logical approach and get the data to set up the possibilities for future, long-term change.

MAKE SURE YOU ARE FOLLOWING YOUR PRINCIPLES

Another rule to being a successful project manager is to follow your principles and the process of project management. In situation after situation, your integrity, ethics, loyalty, and professionalism will be tested or called into question. You must follow your principles to maintain your reputation and to establish yourself as someone who can effect change. If you do not, your lack of principles will become evident.

Here is an example. PMI® is a volunteer-driven, non-profit organization with chapters all over the world. Every chapter has a board of directors that serves on a volunteer basis. These positions are often coveted and sought after, and there are some people who try to assume these positions just to advance their own careers or agendas. When you join PMI® or get certified, you are agreeing to follow a code of ethics. The code of ethics states that the chapter or its events are not to be used to advance personal agendas or promote organizations unless the chapter sponsorship guidelines are followed. Yet there are people who join the board just to get access to the mailing list or to advertise to the members.

Here are some examples of unethical or unacceptable behavior:

- PMI® chapters assign the responsibility of setting up the monthly meetings to the VP of Programs. At his first meeting, one chapter's new VP of Programs passed out a full-page write-up about himself that was in a local newspaper. He also passed out brochures for his training company. His company was not a chapter sponsor.

- In the first month of getting access to the membership list, a new board member began e-mailing the entire membership promotions for his company. His company was not a chapter sponsor.

- A VP of Finance embezzled $50,000 of chapter funds to start up his own business.

These are just a few examples of bad behavior within a single volunteer organization. You can imagine how many more examples there are in companies. But there is one thing to take solace in. For those who insist on taking shortcuts, eventually that behavior catches up with them. People can only take so many shortcuts. They may achieve a temporary gain, but they typically lose in the long run. The litany of corporate scandals that have occurred in recent years is evidence of how a lack of ethics and a lack of integrity will eventually cause individuals' demise. Unfortunately, there may also be many innocent victims. Look at cases like Enron, Tyco, HealthSouth, etc. How many people lost money, jobs, retirement, or their dignity because a few were trying to take a shortcut and get ahead?

In the example of Enron, key executives used mark-to-market accounting practices that allowed them to recognize profits and revenue based on future estimates, offshore accounts, shady side businesses, and insider trading to continuously drive the price of Enron stock up. On paper, it appeared to be an extremely profitable company. Many people were involved in the ruse, including market analysts, banks, regulators, and accountants. In the end, some of the executives made millions of dollars but were also eventually incarcerated. Many people were harmed by their deceit. The famed "Rolling Blackouts" that occurred in California in 2000 and 2001 were promulgated by Enron employees to create an artificial demand and reap huge profits as a result of the deregulation of the power industry in California. Due to a few unscrupulous people, approximately 22,000 people lost their jobs and pensions, and some lost much more. The company's practices put strains on government programs, many Californians lost their homes due to the inability to pay for resources, and many people's lives were changed forever.

Stories such as the Enron downfall and other corporate scandals are cautionary tales that must not be ignored. You must follow your principles. In the end, all you are left with are yourself and your decisions. Can you look at yourself in the mirror and know that you have lived your life with integrity? If not, it is not too late to change. Follow your principles, even when it is hard, and you will reap the rewards.

TAKE CARE OF YOUR TEAM

The work/life balance is one of the hardest things to manage for organizations. Executives want more for less and will continually push the boundaries. In many companies, the nights and weekend work that used to be the exception is becoming the norm. Do we really have to work all of this time? This expectation seems to be prevalent in the United States, but in other countries, this "go, go, go" attitude does not rule the corporate world. I personally witnessed the following example of this concept, which piqued my interest:

I was recently in Italy for a vacation. My family and I were walking down the street in Florence. We saw many kids coming down the street, entering shops, and then the shops closing. This seemed odd because it was 1:30 in the afternoon. On closer inspection, we saw signs with two sets of times for each day in the shop windows. They read:

Aperto: 9 AM – 1:30 PM, 3:30 PM – 7:30 PM

We befriended a shopkeeper and asked about the hours. He explained that in Italy, children generally get out of school at 1:30. So the parents leave work and go home at

1:30 to have lunch as a family and then return afterwards. The family unit is extremely important to Italian culture, as evidenced by the interrupted work day.

My first management job was managing restaurants. I remember being the only restaurant in the area open on Thanksgiving. The corporate office thought it would be a good idea and mandated that we be open. I had to schedule an entire staff to be there, just in case people wanted to eat out. We had two tables all day. I looked around and saw how miserable my staff was. I thought then about what we sacrifice in the hopes of profit. And I saw firsthand that what appears to look good on paper can be devastating to your employees. When I speak in my seminars, I spend time talking about how we need to take care of our people. Our staffs should be the most important thing to us, and achieving the right work/life balance is crucial. I saw this principle taken up a notch in Italy. I think they have it right.

We thanked the shopkeeper and let him get back to his family. I turned and then looked at mine. One of the greatest things I have done this year is take the time to be with them. I bring them with me as much as possible when I travel, but this trip to Italy was different. This time it was just us. There were no schedules or meetings or things that needed to get done. Just us. Just my family. It was what I needed.

We all need to take time for ourselves and our families outside of the work environment. It is essential for our physical and emotional health. But project managers are often the ones who tend to put the pressure on their teams or cause them to be more overworked than the organization's executives. This is because few project managers qualify the dates, really follow the project management process, and fight for their team at every opportunity. Taking care of your team will pay you back tenfold. For those who enjoy their jobs, one of the most cited reasons is that they feel like they are part of a team and that their work is appreciated. Make sure you are taking time to appreciate your team. Make sure you are doing everything you can to balance their work time and their life time. If you do this, they will appreciate you. They will take care of you in kind. It is important to make people your first priority.

TRUST IN YOUR TRAINING

The fourth rule is simple: trust in your training. The project management process works. If you follow it and are true to your profession, success will come your way. Do not become frustrated at the games that companies, sponsors, or team members play. Take each and every opportunity to educate them, show them the reasons behind the process, and help them understand how the process will benefit them. If everyone plays their role appropriately, the entire organization will thrive. The following are some of the benefits different people gain from the use of solid project management and project management processes:

Team Member

- A single list of prioritized work allows each team member to focus on completing his or her activities.

- Reliable estimates show proof of utilization and help achieve a realistic timeline for team members to complete their tasks, which in turn allows the project manager to help protect the work/life balance.

- Proper updates to the project plan help ward off emergencies by allowing the project manager to enact risk mitigation strategies. This again helps protect team members' work/life balance and reduces stress for all involved in the project.

- If project management is done properly, team members need to attend fewer meetings.

Resource Managers

- Estimates for projects can be rolled up to truly see capacity versus demand, which helps ensure resource managers can set realistic expectations for their staff.

- Resource managers will have access to data to help balance cost, resources, and schedule.

- Resource managers can use the data to see whether resources are working outside of their intended roles (e.g., business analysts playing a project management role).

Executives

- Project management provides better data for executives to use in making decisions. When executives work with the project managers, the estimation process can be shortened and the data provided will be much more accurate.

- Organizations can initiate metrics to track even more data for better decisions.

- Good project management will allow the organization to have faith in project estimates.

Project Manager

- A project manager has a chance to truly bring value to the organization by allowing the process to occur.

- Properly updating project management documentation allows for more planning and forward communications.

- The project management process provides proof of time and resources needed for projects; this data can be used in negotiations over schedules and staffing.

- Performing a true what-if analysis allows for a more sophisticated risk management process, which in turn decreases problems and emergency situations on projects.

There are many advantages to following the project process. But it needs to start with you believing in that process. It is not hype. It is not fancy theories that do not mean anything. The project management process is extremely sophisticated and advanced and can help predict the likelihood of future results. So use the process, and trust in your training. This, along with following the other rules laid out in this chapter, will bring you success.

How to Win the Game

You play to win the game!

– Herman Edwards, Head Coach, New York Jets

Herman Edwards said it best. You play to win the game.
The games that have been discussed in this book are
consistently played across organizations. Executives,
team members, and project managers have been engaged
in this behavior for decades. We all know what the games
are, we know the rules of the games, and we know how
to play them. However, we rarely talk frankly about
the games and try to put a stop to them. I'll say it yet
again—it is time for a change. It is time to start having
frank conversations about status, completion dates,
budgets, requirements, and the organization as a whole.
Most employees want to see their companies grow. They
want to see them thrive. But then why do these same
employees continue to play games that are detrimental to
their profession, their organization, and the bottom line?
The answer is that there is a lack of trust and effective
communication.

CRAFTING EFFECTIVE MESSAGES TO BUILD TRUST

Effective communication is the key to successful project management. A project manager should spend from 90 to 95 percent of his or her time communicating on the project. Knowing that you need to communicate is not the same thing as knowing how to communicate, however. There are several key aspects that are important to communications at all levels. Your communications must:

Be Clear

You need to make sure the message you are sending will be interpreted the way you desire. Take all of the unnecessary fluff out of the conversation. We often hear about the "Oreo" method of communicating. This method states that if you have something negative to present, surround it with positive communications. So you say something positive, then you say the statement that you really want to say, and then finish with another positive statement. This method creates noise that sometimes clouds the message, however. And a truly optimistic person will only remember the positive statements and not hear what you really wanted to communicate. Such indirect communication is counterproductive.

Be Concise

Again, too many words can cloud the message. Make sure you are communicating what you are trying to say.

For example, instead of saying, "Certain events outside of our control have impacted us in a way that we did not expect, reflecting in a less than desirable position with regards to our budget," you should say, "Right now, we are over budget."

Be Honest

Stop sugarcoating the responses or trying to lighten the message. If you are over budget or behind schedule, be honest. Present the data in a factual way, and then be honest in giving the options. If you do not know the answer to a question, say so. If you feel that there is something negatively impacting the project, deal with it. Honesty is absolutely the best policy.

Have Actionable Outcomes

Remember to present questions and communications in a way that warrants action. Ask either/or questions versus yes/no questions. Make sure that discussions result in defined action items to complete.

If you follow these rules, you will build trust with your team members. From executives to support personnel, people will begin to trust your word. There is no more powerful trait to have, whether it be in business or in other areas of life, than trustworthiness.

UNDERSTANDING YOUR ROLE

Another important piece involved in stopping the games is understanding your role in the organization. Project managers are facilitators. They analyze information and then present options for outcomes. They are the people who accept the information, digest it, and then formulate communications for all levels of employees to understand. So when running a project, remember—it is not your project! You can own your role as the manager of the project. You can respect the project. But in the end, the project is not yours. It is the sponsor's. The sponsor formally recognized the project and then granted you authority to manage it. The sponsor gave you the budget and the resources to complete the job. Your position is to make sure the budget and resources are adequate to do the work and to present to the sponsor the options for delivery. As discussed earlier in this book, your involvement ends there.

So break free from the bonds and chains of decisions that you did not make! If an executive chooses a poor date and an inadequate budget and then hands the project over to you, you must do everything you can to communicate your concerns about the timeline and funding to your sponsor. But in the end, if you have followed your training, stayed true to project management principles, and appropriately communicated all of the options, then the sponsor is the one who has to live with the decision that he or she made. It is time for project managers to stop losing sleep or being overwhelmed by stress because a project is not going as well as it should. As a project manager, you do not have control over every part of the organization. You cannot force it to mature or to make the right call. But what you can do is set a positive mindset, collect and analyze the data necessary to educate others and present options, and then accept the answers that you are given. Following this process can be truly freeing.

To really drive this point home, let's look at one last example. A project manager was assigned a regulatory project that had to be completed by June 30. If the project was not completed, the company would be fined $1,000,000. The project manager worked with the team to create a plan and realized that under the current resource loading, the project would not be done until October 15. She analyzed options and found that three additional resources were needed to ensure the June 30 date. She approached her sponsor and shared the data. The conversation went as follows:

> **PM:** "We just finished planning this project and have a big decision to make."

> **Sponsor:** "What is that?"

> **PM:** "In order to complete this project on time, we need three additional resources. If we do not get the resources, we are likely to absorb the fine."

Sponsor: "We do not have three resources to give you. Do it with fewer people or make the team work harder."

PM: "Sir, we can look at that as an option, but we run the risk of turnover by demanding the type of hours that you are asking them to work."

Sponsor: "If they want their jobs, they will do it."

PM: "OK. We will do our best, but to be clear, instead of adding the three resources that we have identified as necessary to be successful, you want us to do it with existing staff."

Sponsor: "That is what I said."

In this situation, the project manager knew that even if she fought harder, she was not going to convince the sponsor. And there was nobody else to escalate the issue to. However, she had a sense of peace about her because she knew that the decision was made. She and the team worked as hard as they could to deliver the project on time. Two of the key resources quit during the project and cited the lack of work/life balance as the cause. It was too late in the project to bring new people on. Ultimately, they missed the date and incurred the $1,000,000 fine. Then the following conversation took place:

Sponsor: "How could we miss that project?"

PM: "We ran out of time."

Sponsor: "You should have made everyone work harder!"

PM: "Sir, with all due respect, we said that this was going to happen. We needed three resources, and in lieu of receiving them, we pushed everyone to the hilt. We identified the risk of people leaving under that pressure and that occurred. We did our best."

Sponsor: "So you are saying this is my fault?"

PM: "No sir; I am saying that I should have done a better job showing you that we really needed those resources to be successful. How can I present that information better next time so that we have more options than we had on this project?"

In this example, the project manager did let the sponsor off the hook a bit, but it created an opportunity for them to have an open and honest conversation about what had occurred. Such conversations are necessary. The negotiations with sponsors are extremely important, and they should not be taken lightly. A lot of other people are impacted by these negotiations—those that have occurred and those that will occur in the future. Remember, although a project may be considered a failure, there may still have been a whole team of people who sacrificed nights and weekends to try to pull the initiative off. However, the most comprehensive data and the best presentation skills in the world cannot prevent every poor decision. When poor decisions are made, you have to recognize where the responsibility lies for the decision and let the chains of worry drop away. You role is to facilitate, not make all of the decisions.

BECOME A REAL PROJECT MANAGER!

It is time to make a decision. You either believe in the processes and fundamentals of project management or you do not. We are nearing the end of this book. If you are reading this last section, then it is probably safe to assume you have already made that decision. Now it is time to reflect on what you have read. Reflect on the points you have agreed with and those you have disagreed with. It is time to start applying the principles that you have been taught and practicing the art form that is project management. Not everyone can do it. Not everyone can be successful at it. However, if you are honest, if you are true to yourself, and if you follow the principles of project management, it really can be a rewarding career. In fact, it is one of the best career paths out there. As a project manager, your job is to facilitate the creation of something new, be it a new product, feature, service, or process. The result of your project never existed before in your organization. Through your work, you are changing what is "normal" and bringing a new venture or new ideas to realization. The project management profession can expose you to many new things and processes, and your skills are portable. Although there is much debate about this idea, if you are an expert in project management, you do not necessarily have to be an expert in specific industries. They have tons of experts already. Your job is to mine their knowledge and make them achieve things they did not think were possible.

So make the decision. Follow the path. Become a real project manager. Sleep at night. Enjoy your job. Maintain your own work/life balance. Be at peace with the process. Educate your executives. Educate your team. Be an advocate for the profession. Affix a positive connotation to the work that you do. And by doing so, realize your dreams and goals, and achieve what you once felt was impossible. Do not wait for tomorrow. Make the decision now to be a real project manager. There is a whole world out there that is in desperate need of you and your skills.